ANY CAMERA
ANYWHERE

THE NEW STREET PHOTOGRAPHER'S MANIFESTO

ANY CAMERA ANYWHERE

THE NEW STREET PHOTOGRAPHER'S MANIFESTO

TANYA NAGAR

ilex

An Hachette UK Company www.hachette.co.uk

First published in Great Britain in 2012 by
ILEX, a division of Octopus Publishing Group Ltd
Octopus Publishing Group
Carmelite House
50 Victoria Embankment
London, EC4Y 0DZ
www.octopusbooks.co.uk

Publisher: Alastair Campbell
Associate Publisher: Adam Juniper
Managing Editor: Natalia Price-Cabrera
Editor: Tara Gallagher
Specialist Editor: Frank Gallaugher
Creative Director: James Hollywell
Senior Designer: Kate Haynes
Designer: Jon Allen
Picture Manager: Katie Greenwood
Senior Production Manager: Peter Hunt

ISBN 978-1-908150-46-2

A CIP catalogue record for this book is available from the British Library

Printed and bound in China

10 9 8 7 6 5 4 3

CONTENTS

INTRODUCTION

The New Street Photographer's Manifesto aims to inspire and equip you with the knowledge you need to be able to go out onto the streets and immortalize moments of life, with whichever camera you choose to use.

In this book we will cover the use of traditional tools, as well as venturing into modern-day technology, and popular mobile phone cameras.

I am a firm believer that street photography should not be limited to those with expensive gear; through experimentation and practice you will find what works for you as a photographer. The key is to explore the different options available, and to discover and develop your own personal style—both in terms of equipment and in terms of your method of shooting.

For example, some people exclusively shoot with a digital SLR, while others prefer to use only film. No one method is better than the other, although they will differ depending on the camera you are using. The New Street Photographer's Manifesto will highlight these differences and help you decide what you enjoy most. Ultimately, you the photographer will decide what camera you prefer working with, and you can nurture your skills with your chosen equipment over time.

The last chapter in the book is a "showcase" section, featuring some of the most inspirational and talented street photographers around the world today. Each photographer discusses their approach to street photography, and deconstructs the shooting process behind a favorite image, providing unique and personal insights into how they shoot.

Remember, street photography is accessible to us all; you do not need special equipment or fancy locations to create a great street photograph—that is the beauty of street photography, anyone, anywhere can capture a moment in time.

→ **Bicycle Men—Jinja, Uganda**
Canon EOS 350D, 18–55mm ƒ/3.5–5.6 lens
These men were having a chat on their bikes, and as I walked past them they all looked up at me, and I captured that very moment. As soon as I lowered my camera they asked me why I had taken their picture, and protested at being photographed. I explained the essence of street photography and how if I had asked for permission from them it would have ruined the moment. We had a discussion for a few minutes about street photography, and they felt appeased by the end of it.

Street photography can be an alien concept to many, so educating your subjects can help them to understand your philosophy, and why you're capturing these kind of candid moments. Of course, in some situations people simply won't be interested, so respect that and move on. Don't dwell on any negative reactions or let them hinder your street photography.

1.
STREET
PHOTOGRAPHY

Camera + Moment + Precision + Perfect timing = Street Photograph

WHAT IS STREET PHOTOGRAPHY?

Street is a unique genre of photography. It doesn't depend on hours of planning, expensive or elaborate gear, or fashionable, and trendy locations. It simply requires a camera, an eye for moments and perfect timing in everyday and often mundane surroundings, accessible to everyone, anywhere.

It is in those seemingly banal surroundings that moments of expression, beauty, and social interaction can be found in abundance. Look long enough and you'll see it all around you—a taxi driver waiting for his next customer, a woman on the train, a homeless man crossing the road. These ordinary moments that encompass everyday life can produce fascinating, humoros, and profound reflections of the human world in which we live.

Despite the apparent simplicity of street photography, it would be imprudent to underestimate the skill involved in capturing these fleeting scenes. The world is in constant motion all around us. Blink, and the moment is lost forever. In order to photograph these once-in-a-lifetime moments, you have to be ready to pounce and seize the opportunity, while simultaneously attempting to compose the shot and look inconspicuous.

Similar to documentary photography or photojournalism, street photography is about capturing the reality of our surroundings—candid moments that could be lost in a flash. Unlike many other forms of photography, you cannot plan a moment, or retake the same scene numerous times in search of perfection. There is simply no time for this. You can anticipate and predict, but in essence street is about observation, timing, and precision. Master these traits, and you will be positively surprised and impressed at the results.

The aim of the *The New Street Photographer's Manifesto* is to bring you closer to the world; to capture fragments of life that once gone, may never return, whatever camera you have, wherever you are.

The subjects of street photography are all around us and not limited to the street, but rather the public domain in general with people going about their daily lives. Immerse yourself in the urban world with your camera as your companion, and you'll start seeing the world in a new and exciting light.

→ **Ask this Man—London, UK**
Nikon EM, 50mm *f*/1.8 lens, Ilford XP2 Super 400 film
This image was shot in Camden, a bustling area of London famous for punks, grunge, music, and fashion. To me, this image represents Camden in its entirety, and the eye contact engages the viewer with the subject.

↑ Taxi driver—Mumbai, India

Canon EOS 350D, 18–55mm ƒ/3.5–5.6 lens

It was late at night and I noticed this taxi driver waiting for his next customer. Taxis in Mumbai very often have interesting characteristics. In this case, the plastic grapes hanging from the mirror, and the atmospheric lighting, along with the serene look on the driver's face prompted me to capture this moment. How many of us would find inspiration in a taxi driver? If you open your eyes enough you will begin to spot details in scenes that you may ordinarily ignore.

↑ Stuart—London, UK

Canon EOS 350D, 50mm ƒ/1.8 lens

I followed this man for a while as he crossed the road, and when he sat down on a bench I approached him and we had a conversation about why he's walking around the city with a blanket in this way. I was apprehensive at first as I thought he would act in a hostile manner—a stereotypical assumption about a homeless man. However, I was surprised to learn that he chooses this way of life, and he let me take some portraits of him. His name is Stuart.

THE HISTORY OF STREET PHOTOGRAPHY

The concept of what we refer to as "street" photography can be dated as far back as the early 1800s, when photography was still in its infancy. People began experimenting with and exploring a new exciting medium that could freeze time and immortalize moments forever.

However, it was in the late 1930s that a French photojournalist named Henri Cartier-Bresson adopted the idea of capturing candid images of life around him. He would venture out with a light-weight and portable Leica rangefinder camera with a fast 50mm lens, and free from bulky equipment capture the ebb and flow of the world around him. The Leica became his camera of choice and accompanied him everywhere. The portability, agility, and speed of this camera allowed Cartier-Bresson to capture what he called the "decisive moment," an expression that has become synonymous with his work, and one that is referred to regularly in the world of street photography.

Cartier-Bresson believed that every image should be taken at a "decisive moment"—when aspects of the photograph should come together to form a moment that tells a story.

Cartier-Bresson's philosophy on street photography included shooting in black and white, with a rangefinder camera, and without the use of flash. He was a true believer in creating the image exclusively within the camera as opposed to post-processing/manipulating in the dark room, and was inconspicuous in his approach—weaving quickly along the streets, in search of the decisive moment. His technique and views on street photography propelled Henri Cartier-Bresson to legendary status as a photographer and pioneer of street, and his photos have become some of the most iconic images known today.

Along with Cartier-Bresson, many others such as Robert Doisneau adopted similar methodologies and principles. People were beginning to use photography as a means to record society, seeing the potential of what could be captured through the lens of their camera on the everyday streets with everyday people.

← Leica M6
This "classic" style of street photography involving black-and-white film and a rangefinder camera gave this genre its signature look; today, purists of street photography would argue their methods are what make street photography, street photography.

**↑ Henri Cartier-Bresson. ROMANIA.
In a train. 1975.**
Credit © Henri Cartier-Bresson/Magnum Photos.

STREET PHOTOGRAPHY TODAY

Times have changed since the 1930s. Cameras are no longer limited to the wealthy elite; nor are they restricted to physical film.

Today there are countless types of camera, ones to suit every budget and requirement. For example, most of us carry a camera without even subconsciously thinking we are, in the form of our mobile phone. It might not conform to the traditionalist viewpoint of street, but as basic as this camera may seem, phone photography (phoneography) is an ever-growing and popular form of the art.

Technology has allowed us to do away with film. We no longer have to wait for pictures to be processed and developed. It just takes a click and within a moment we can upload images to share with others, something that was unthinkable in the 1930s. The digital medium has also meant that photography has become cheaper.

Color photography has also become popular, changing the "look" of street photography. It has developed the landscape of street photography by bringing bright, vibrant street images to the table.

In short, we now have a vast range of equipment choices suitable for every conceivable budget. While we can still employ the same methods as the founding fathers of street photography and use a rangefinder with black-and-white film, we now also have the option of digital SLRs,

mobile phone cameras and compact digital cameras, among many others. Despite technology moving forward providing an array of possibilities, the principles of street photography have remained the same—to capture the "decisive moment."

↑ Riot of Color—Haridwar, India
Canon EOS 350D, 24–70mm f/2.8 lens
A demonstration of the power of color, and how it can be used to produce visually engaging images, fully representative of the real world in which the image was shot.

↓ ATM—Dublin, Ireland
Sony Ericsson D750i
An image shot with a basic 2 megapixel (MP) Sony camera phone. Camera phones can have much higher resolution than this—the iPhone 4S, for example, features an 8MP camera.

THE MIND OF THE STREET PHOTOGRAPHER

Before we begin to talk about methods and shooting techniques of street photography, it's important to discuss the mindset of the street photographer. I have met numerous photographers who all engage in various styles of shooting, using different cameras. However, all successful street photographers have one fundamental trait in common—lack of fear.

It is fear that causes hesitation to capture the moment. If you think twice, the moment will be gone—lost forever. In many cases there is no time to waste, and hesitation, fed by fear, causes this.

Conquer your fear!

Let's think of street photography as hunting.

> **Street photographer = Hunter**
> **The "decisive moment" = Capturing the prey**

A hunter has no time to hesitate, and if he/she feels scared, they cannot let it show as the prey will sense the fear, and use it to their advantage and escape, or perhaps even attack. As a street photographer you are like a hunter; attentive, agile, and quick to capture the moment before it escapes from the grips of your camera. If you hesitate for just one second, before you know it the moment will have disappeared, and you will be left holding your camera, without your prize. We will look at ways in which to be unobtrusive and blend into the background like a hunter, but whether you are shooting openly, within clear sight of the subject, or are unseen, you mustn't hesitate. It is the one flaw that will cause you to make, at best, average photos.

Fear of what?

Today's society is paranoid more than ever of being captured on camera. As a photographer, you must be conscious of social norms and be sensitive to those you might be shooting, particularly when dealing with the likes of children and the vulnerable, for example. By the same token, being too cautious will mean you will constantly be worrying about what people think of you. As a result, you will not be able to capture images freely as your mind will be occupied with fear—fear of what the subject may think, say, or do if they see you point your camera at them.

Smile!

Practically every street photographer at some time or another will be on the receiving end of hostility. But any hostility can be appeased by one very simple gesture—a smile. In my experience, smiling breaks down the barrier between subject and photographer. It's the simple psychology of human behavior and interaction, the fundamentals in fact of street photography.

→ **Biker Boy—Zurich, Switzerland**
Nikon F3, 50mm ƒ/1.8 lens, Kodak Ultramax 400 film
I spotted this man taking a smoke on his bike, overlooking the river. I shot an image from the back, and then as I walked past I decided to shoot him face-on. As I composed and focused, he looked up and spotted me. At first I wasn't sure if he was angry as he remained serious, as though he was wondering why I was shooting him. I smiled at him, and he smiled back—a sign that he was okay with being photographed. The tension immediately disappeared after this simple, natural gesture.

Here are some dos and don'ts to get you into the right frame of mind when photographing the streets.

Do:
- Be courageous! As a photographer you have the right to be out and about with your camera. It is no big deal—do not lose sight of this.
- Smile if seen. This will in most cases break down any barriers and put the subject at ease.
- Know the law and what your rights are (see page 69).
- Talk to the subject if necessary. Explain why you took the picture if the reaction appears to be hostile. In most cases the subject will be interested in hearing what you have to say. Humans are curious, and the majority of the time, they just want to know more. Street photography can be an alien subject to many, so educating your subjects can help them understand where you're coming from and why you're capturing these kinds of candid moments. Of course, in some situations people simply won't be interested, so respect that and move onto the next moment. Don't dwell on any negative reactions or let them hinder you.
- Respect your subjects. If someone objects to being photographed, respect their decision.
- Stay calm. Your aim is to capture the "decisive moment." If you're agitated, worried or nervous, this could have a negative effect.
- Take (reasonable) risks to get an interesting shot. If you see the potential for a great moment, chase it!

Don't:
- Put your well being at risk and take pictures of something that could cause you physical harm.
- Argue or be rude. This will make the situation worse. Calmly walk away if necessary.
- Invade someone's personal space by being obtrusive and sticking your camera into their face. You don't want to annoy people, and all you will do is capture someone provoked by your camera, and that's not representative of street photography.
- Break the law. Remember, in most parts of the world you have the right to be in the public domain with your camera. I can't emphasize this enough. If you are traveling, exercise caution, and adapt to the local customs and culture. Know what is acceptable and what is not.

← Speak to the Hand—London, UK
Canon EOS 350D, 50mm *f*/1.8 lens
Reactions such as this are not uncommon, but with the right approach can sometimes be avoided. In other instances people will be adamant about not being photographed, and in those cases, it is best to simply walk away.

The street photographer is inquisitive, observant, and has the courage to shoot scenes of strangers, even while among strangers. As with most skills, practice makes perfect. If you're scared initially, go out accompanied by a friend or someone else. Try wearing headphones—people are less likely to approach you if you appear to be listening to music.

Whatever the case, over time you will start to shoot without hesitation—timeliness is everything, so eliminate the fear. It is all part of the challenge and excitement. With the right attitude you will find street photography an enjoyable and exciting adventure!

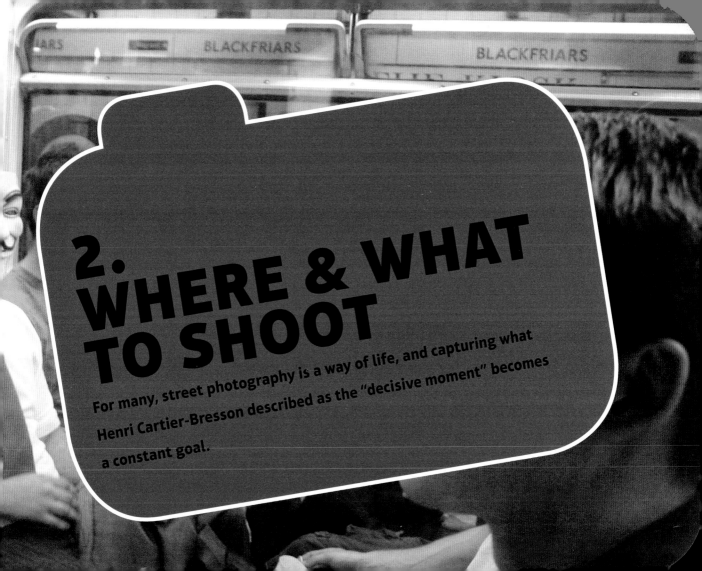

2.
WHERE & WHAT TO SHOOT

For many, street photography is a way of life, and capturing what Henri Cartier-Bresson described as the "decisive moment" becomes a constant goal.

SETTING THE SCENE—LOCATION

As any seasoned street photographer will tell you, there will be times when you deeply regret not having your camera on you, and once you develop an eye for moments, you will have a burning desire to capture them via your lens.

The whole essence of street photography is that, like human behavior, moments are unpredictable, spontaneous and elusive. Therefore having your camera with you at all times ensures that you have the opportunity to capture them, and won't regret the dreaded missed opportunity, which will inevitably occur!

Locations needn't be predetermined or planned in advance. A major advantage of street photography is that it is not limited in terms of locations or subjects—the possibilities are endless. Wherever there is a "moment," there is a photo to be made—in cities, in suburbia, on public transport, in parks—the list just doesn't stop. The best street photographers are flexible, quick to adapt and to blend into the surroundings.

Over the next few pages we'll examine some key locations and explore their characteristics.

↑ **Monks—London, UK**
Canon EOS 350D, 50mm ƒ/1.8 lens
This image was shot at a pro-Burma protest that many monks had attended. I spo
these two monks taking a picture of the crowds, and noticed how they were both
dressed and poised similarly. Protests can provide a great backdrop for images, a
shooting at such an event requires less inconspicuous behavior as many others w
also be capturing their own moments, and you will easily blend into the crowd.

TIP
If you initially have a fear of being out and about with your camera, then start with public events such as protests or parades. They create the ideal opportunity in which to build up confidence and to experiment freely without being worried about being spotted. Cafés are also great places to people-watch while sitting in a relaxing atmosphere; they provide a lot of activity and innumerable expressions.

Crowded locations

City centers—shopping centers (malls), markets, cafés

Popular tourist spots

Beaches

Parks

Public events such as parades and protests

Public transport and roads

In all these locations it's "easy" to blend in with a camera, as there may be many other people taking photographs. In these surroundings it is less important to be inconspicuous as you will not be drawing attention to yourself. In fact, taking pictures in these places may well be the norm, in which case you'll be able to shoot openly without any fear of being spotted.

However, there are exceptions to the rule. A packed train or elevator, for example, while full of people, are not places you'd usually be photographing in. So you still need to be unobtrusive as the distance between you, the photographer, and the subject is much closer than is normally the case between strangers.

Shooting on a packed train requires a different method of shooting compared with say, walking around a busy and noisy zoo with a camera at the ready.

↑ **Holi—Mumbai, India**
Canon EOS 350D, 18–55mm *f*/3.5–5.6 lens
All kinds of activities take place on the beach. In this case, the Hindu festival of Holi was ongoing, and I captured these boys running around and celebrating. Be aware of festivals or events as they can provide some fun and new scenarios.

↑ **Masks on the Tube—London, UK**
Canon EOS 350D, 18–55mm *f*/3.5–5.6 lens
I captured this moment after a protest, where masked campaigners got onto a train. Trains can provide a sea of possibilities in terms of characters and behaviors. Just before the train pulled away I spotted four of the masked campaigners all sitting next to each other staring straight ahead.

↑ Prayers in the Park—London, UK
Canon EOS 350D, 100mm ƒ/2.8 lens
Parks can be interesting places. While they are mostly associated with picnics, benches, and joggers, there are often other activities taking place that might not seem as obvious initially. These Muslim men appeared to spontaneously pray on the grass as a man walked past, almost as though it is a regular occurrence. Perhaps here it is.

↑ Funland—Dublin, Ireland
Nikon FM, 50mm ƒ/1.8 lens, Kodak 400CN film
There is always a hub of activity on the streets, and if you look around enough you'll spot moments that are unusual or seem out of place compared to the norm.

Quiet locations

Suburbia—quiet streets

Rural areas

Museums

Libraries

The location or setting can be just as important as the subject, as it puts the subject into context. An image is a whole entity and each frame must be treated as such; pay attention and be observant to what is visible in the frame.

↗ Seagull and Pint—Jersey, UK
Canon EOS 350D, 18–55mm ƒ/3.5–5.6 lens
A somewhat abstract scene featuring part of a seagull, and an empty pint glass—the only signs of life in what was an otherwise deserted street.

↑ Jesus Wins—Jinja, Uganda
Canon EOS 350D, 18–55mm ƒ/3.5–5.6 lens
I was walking down a quiet suburban road when I came across this child peering through a door, smiling at me, even before I lifted up my camera to compose. The combination of the child, the position of the opening, and the sticker prompted me to capture this moment.

THINK OUTSIDE THE BOX

Some of the places and locations we covered earlier are obvious, while others are not. Think creatively—street photography doesn't necessarily have to have you literally out and about on the streets.

While traveling around India, I found that I spent a lot of my time stuck in traffic jams, or on public transport. So, naturally, I began shooting from within vehicles, and it opened up a whole new world and perspectives that I hadn't previously considered, with just a pane of glass separating me from the subjects.

→ **Sleeping Men—Mumbai, India**
Canon EOS 350D, 18–55mm ƒ/3.5–5.6 lens
People sleeping on the streets of Mumbai is a common sight, and I spotted this scene from a distance and got my camera ready and in position for when the car I was in passed them.

← Car Beggar—Mumbai, India

Canon EOS 350D, 18–55mm *f*/3.5–5.6 lens

Beggars in India do not hesitate to approach taxis and to reach into them to ask for money. This is a sight I was initially unaccustomed to, but one I was lucky enough to capture here.

↓ Boy Selling Flags—Mumbai, India

Canon EOS 350D, 24–70mm *f*/2.8 lens

This boy was moving from car to car in heavy traffic selling plastic flags for a rupee each. I wanted to buy one and as he reached into the window to hand me the flag, I composed and shot. He took his money and wandered off to try and sell to the next person, carrying on with his life as usual.

↑ Dhobi Ghat—Mumbai, India
Canon EOS 350D, 24–70mm *f*/2.8 lens
This is Asia's largest open-air laundry, visible from a
bridge. This shot illustrates the hustle and bustle of
this busy place where clothes from all over the city
are brought to be washed, dried, and ironed.

The bigger picture
When exploring new places,
or even old ones, think about
the bigger picture. Images of
entire places from afar can
create striking scenes.

Yes, street is partly
about getting among your
subjects, up close and
personal, but a wider
perspective can enable
you to capture the ambience
of a location.

WHAT MAKES A GREAT PHOTO?

We have now established that street photography is about capturing candid and spontaneous moments of life, but what exactly is a "moment." What are we looking for?

A moment can be defined as:
1) A short indefinite period/point of time.
2) A specific instance.

What's so special about a moment?

Like any art form, street photography is subjective and about your own personal observations. You are capturing life as you see it—authentic, real, and raw moments that perhaps most people would miss.

It could represent a state such as irony, humor, love, or contradiction. It could evoke an emotion such as sadness or anger. Start looking around you and begin to observe people in your surroundings. You will start to develop an eye for such moments and you will be surprised at just how many worthy captures there could be in what others may consider mundane scenes.

→ **Asleep—Tokyo, Japan**
Canon EOS 350D, 24–70mm ƒ/2.8 lens
A woman asleep on the Tokyo metro.

USING "PROPS"

There are a number of factors that can produce striking images. Here are some things to look out for when searching for that frame-worthy moment.

The "street" is not a blank canvas. There are numerous elements that make up our surroundings, and these elements can be thought of as "props." The use of street props can help make an image stand out and accentuate certain details of the scene, as well as play a more central role to the subjects involved. If used successfully, these additional aspects can be used to the street photographer's advantage. What it takes is an eye to recognize them.

Graffiti and signage
One example where such so-called props provide a visually engaging capture is the use of graffiti, signs, and graphical billboards. Graffiti is a common man-made element found in cities and urban landscapes, and while the beauty of such art can be debatable, there is no doubt that it can provide a striking backdrop to a scene.

Words, text, and advertising
Text and advertising logos can also be used effectively within a scene, particularly where it may relate directly to the subjects captured in the frame.

↑ **Denied the Right to Move—London, UK**
Canon EOS 350D, 18–55mm ƒ/3.5–5.6 lens
Taken during a protest, I found the juxtaposition of the words and their meaning surrounded by the feet of bystanders quite fitting.

↑ If Only—Jerusalem, Israel

Canon EOS 350D, 18–55mm ƒ/3.5–5.6 lens
What compelled me to take this photo was the irony and almost farcical placement of a soldier's gun pointing to the world-famous golden arches of one of the largest and well-known corporations in the Western world. This is an example of where an image is not simply an image, but through the use of advertising and literally a prop (in this case the gun) it takes on a deeper meaning.

↗ Big Brother—London, UK

Canon EOS 350D, 18–55mm ƒ/3.5–5.6 lens
In essence this is simply a man walking down the road. However, the large eye plays an integral and fundamental role in the execution of the photo, and turns an ordinary scene into something extraordinary.

→ Exclamation—London, UK

Canon EOS 350D, 18–55mm ƒ/3.5–5.6 lens
This image was taken at a protest where there were many bespoke hand-made signs being used. Here an exclamation mark coupled with a man on the phone and a pair of legs create a somewhat abstract composition.

CONTRASTS & SIMILARITIES

Stark contrasts as well as uncanny similarities within an image will always stand out, as they make us ponder, think and smile, rather than simply being a "nice" picture. As you begin to open your eyes to your surroundings you will start to notice contrasting and conflicting moments.

Contrasts can work on either a visual or metaphorical level. Here are some of the more obvious contrasts you're likely to come across—light versus dark, big versus small, rich versus poor.

← **Trio—London, UK**
Nikon EM, 24mm *f*/2 lens, Agfa APX 100 film
Three unrelated tourists stand together in the same pose.

↑ **Balloon Girls—London, UK**
Canon EOS 350D, 18–55mm *f*/3.5–5.6 lens
An example of stark contrasts often found in many large cities.

EYE CONTACT

Street photography is about candid and unposed moments. If a subject makes eye contact, does this mean it is not street photography since the subject is aware of being photographed? Not necessarily, no.

People look at each other—this is natural behavior. If a subject looks at you while you have your lens aimed at them, and they smile, they are naturally reacting to you, and as such this is not predetermined behavior, but a spontaneous moment of interaction between photographer and subject.

Eye contact is powerful and it takes courage to make an image of a stranger while they are looking directly at you or into your lens. Take advantage of such a situation, as it will, in most cases, produce an effective and poignant frame.

In the examples of eye contact shown here, the subjects did not react or adapt their behavior. It's almost as though they didn't notice or realize they were being captured on camera, despite looking straight into the lens.

↗ Man On Train—London, UK
Canon EOS 350D, 24–70mm ƒ/2.8 lens
Taken on the day Prince William married Kate Middleton. London was full of revellers celebrating.

↑ Monsoon Girl—Mumbai, India
Canon EOS 350D, 18–55mm ƒ/3.5–5.6 lens
This girl peered through the window of the car I was traveling in. She didn't react or move when I lifted up my camera to capture her, despite the close proximity of subject and camera. This kind of occurrence is common in Mumbai where people often seem to ignore the camera while looking right into it.

MOMENTS WITHOUT HUMANS

A frame does not necessarily have to show people in it for it to be a street photograph. What you are doing is capturing human life, and remnants of such life are all around us, even if the people themselves have long since moved on.

The urban environment we live in provides a variety of objects to capture that depict signs of human interaction and existence, such a litter for example.

↑ **Human Necessities—Palestine**
Canon EOS 350D, 24–70mm ƒ/2.8 lens
Just moments before, one can only imagine that three Arabs stood in the afternoon sunshine talking over these cups of coffee.

← **Dead Bear—Surrey, UK**
Nikon F3, 50mm ƒ/1.8 lens, Kodak 200 film
A bear abandoned in the street with its insides strewn across the pavement.

ANIMALS

Animals such as pets are often an integral aspect of society (for example pets or certain livestock), and as such can feature heavily in street photography.

Like humans, animals are unpredictable and their behavior can be a challenge to photograph. You must still remain quick and agile when photographing animals to ensure you capture the desired moment.

↗ **Portrait of a Dog—Tokyo, Japan**
Canon EOS 350D, 24–70mm ƒ/2.8 lens
Shot in the nick of time, just as the dog raised its paw.

→ **Dog in the Street—Surrey, UK**
Nikon F3, 50mm ƒ/1.8 lens, Kodak 200 film
A dog sits on the sidewalk, appearing to pose naturally for the camera.

ATTENTION TO DETAIL

Always be on the lookout for the finer details—the details that are not so apparent immediately, but that on further inspection contain elements that are interesting, or worthy of a "decisive moment."

In order to spot these you will have to open your eyes even further and learn to zone in on your surroundings. Drill down into the bigger picture and begin to appreciate the moments most people would never care to observe. This will set you apart from those simply taking snapshots.

↑ Green and Gold—Mumbai, India
Canon EOS 350D, 18–55mm ƒ/3.5–5.6 lens
Looking up I noticed the richness of gold and green adorning every arm.

← 1 Trick Lane—London, UK
Canon EOS 350D, 50mm ƒ/1.8 lens
Brick Lane is a prominent street in East London, and I noticed the street sign has been cleverly transformed into "1 Trick Lane." Graffiti is constantly evolving and as with people, such moments can easily disappear as fast as they first appeared.

THE UNUSUAL IN THE USUAL

Street photography is not necessarily just about capturing ordinary, everyday moments. Keep your eyes open for the more unusual goings on that would make for some funny or amusing captures that perhaps you wouldn't ordinarily see, but which still take place in the environment around you.

↑ Dog with Sunglasses—Istanbul, Turkey
Leica M6, 35mm ƒ/1.4 lens, Kodak Ultramax 400 film
A man traveling around Istanbul on a scooter with a dog sporting sunglasses. It was a bizarre sight and I had to run to catch up with them in order to get this shot before they disappeared down the street.

← Masked and Policeman—London, UK
Canon EOS 350D, 18–55mm ƒ/3.5–5.6 lens
I spotted this slightly odd moment meters away from a protest. This kind of strange sighting is more common than you may first think, particularly in larger towns and cities where there are all kinds of characters and personas in the public domain. Keep your eyes open and your camera ready at all times to capture them.

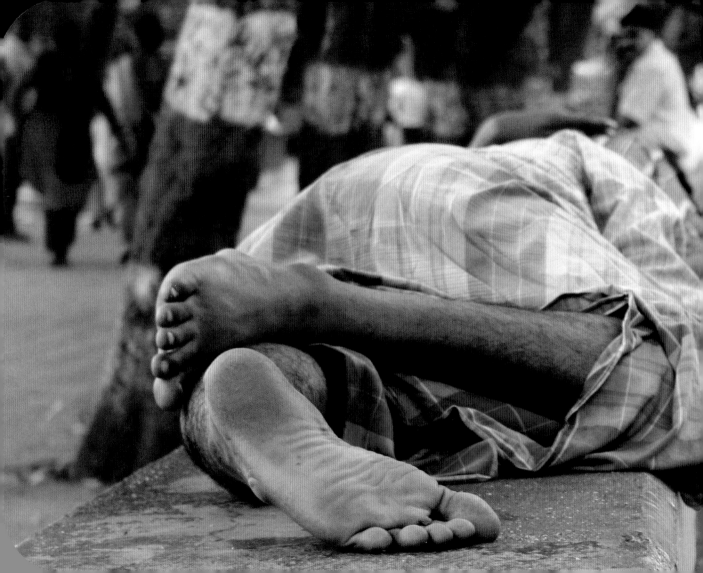

3.
SEIZE THE
MOMENT

Observe then react—seize every opportunity.

TIMING

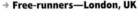

By now you should have a good idea of what makes an impact. How are you going to capture this? You could simply point and shoot, but effective photographs that make a statement in some way often require more than just a bit of luck.

The key ingredient is in timing. I cannot emphasize how important this aspect of street photography is. The only way you will be able to be quick at shooting is if you get to grips with your camera and know exactly how it works. Through practice you will become proficient at using your camera, and therefore quicker at shooting, ensuring you will not lose time fiddling with settings. Every second is valuable.

Before you do anything, remove the lens cap and keep it off. It sounds obvious, but it is a common mistake. Being out and about so much will no doubt cause wear and tear to your equipment. As a safeguard, put a UV filter onto your lens to protect it instead.

→ **Free-runners—London, UK**
Canon EOS 350D, 10–22mm ƒ/3.5–4.5 lens
Here is an illustration of how accurate timing can "make" an image. I stumbled across a group of free-runners in central London who were practicing *parkour*, which involves running and climbing on buildings. I watched them for a while and as soon as the main subject did a handstand I composed and clicked. The result of this frame was a mixture of luck, opportunity, observation, and crucially, precise timing.

COMPOSITION

Composition is concerned with the placing of the subjects within the frame. How and where will you place the subject within the frame so that it creates the most impact?

The center
The viewer's eyes are naturally drawn to central parts of a picture, making this a distinct place for the subject to stand out.

Symmetry
Be attentive to symmetrical scenes, shapes, and patterns that could make interesting juxtapositions within the frame.

↗ **Dhobi Ghat—Mumbai, India**
Canon EOS 350D, 24–70mm ƒ/2.8 lens
The Dhobi Ghat is an outdoor laundry, and in this case there is only one subject. The drops of water in the air almost act as though they are framing the workman, so I chose to place him centrally, enveloped by the droplets.

→ **Benched—Zurich, Switzerland**
Nikon F3, 50mm ƒ/1.8 lens, Kodak Ultramax 400 film
An ordinary scene in a busy street is made more interesting by using the positions of people within the frame.

Rule of thirds

The rule of thirds dictates that a frame should be split into nine sections, with the main subject(s) placed along the lines or at the intersections. The sections should contain three lines spaced equally, horizontally, and vertically. Ideally, the main subject would be positioned in a space the size of one third of the frame, or at least off-set, instead of slap bang in the middle.

The idea is that off-setting the subject in this way provides more interest and character within the frame than simply centering it, and particularly when it comes to portraits, the rule of thirds is an effective one.

↗ **Smoking Man—Haridwar, India**
Canon EOS 350D, 24–70mm ƒ/2.8 lens
This rickshaw driver was waiting for his next customer, and he lit a cigarette and looked toward me. I felt compelled to capture him, and composed using the rule of thirds, framed by the rickshaws.

→ **Halil—Istanbul, Turkey**
Leica M6, 35mm ƒ/1.4 lens, Kodak Ultramax 400 film
This boy stood in this position for a few moments, and when I raised my camera to shoot him, he didn't move or react in any way.

⬇ **Monkey on a Leash—Delhi, India**
Canon EOS 350D, 18–55mm ƒ/3.5–5.6 lens
This performing monkey stared right into my lens. Again,
the rule of thirds was used to draw attention not only to
the main subject, but to the partially visible men around.

Shooting portraits

In terms of portraits, an easy mistake to make is inadvertently cutting off the feet. These images could have been great—both were shot on film and at the time of taking them I was not aware that I'd chopped the feet off. It was only when the images were developed that I realized my mistake.

If you're capturing a full-length portrait then make it an entire full-length portrait. Cutting feet off can ruin a photo and can turn what could have been a great image into more of an amateur snapshot.

↗ Street Sweeper—Ankara, Turkey

Leica M6, 35mm f/1.4 lens, Kodak ColorPlus 200 film
I spotted this cleaner from afar and had planned to shoot him while he worked. As I approached him I got ready to compose, but he stopped to take a break and let me pass. He didn't react as I pointed the camera at him, but unfortunately in a rush to take the frame, I didn't compose in the best possible way.

→ Accordion Player—Vienna, Austria

Nikon F3, 50mm f/1.8 lens, Ilford XP2 Super 400 film
This busker continued to perform as I stood in front of him to take this. Street performers are quite likely used to people taking photos of them; be bold and don't be afraid to shoot facing them full-on, but think about the composition. Again, this photo could have been much better had I kept the feet in the frame.

Framing and juxtaposition

Juxtaposition is the positioning of elements next to one another. Frame the subject you are photographing by using the surroundings, whether these are objects, other people or light sources. You can use factors within the scene to draw attention to the subject itself.

↗ Woman at Gig—London, UK
Canon EOS 350D, 18–55mm ƒ/3.5–5.6 lens
The woman in the center of the image is framed by the silhouettes of two men on either side of the picture. Furthermore, the light is striking and appears to be firmly on her, acting as a spotlight, drawing attention to her. Yet she is oblivious to being caught on camera and simply immersed in her book.

→ Haji Ali Singers—Mumbai, India
Canon EOS 350D, 24–70mm ƒ/2.8 lens
What you see here are men who spend the day singing religious songs near a mosque in India. Local people generally ignore them and walk passed, in the same way as the homeless are often ignored. This image depicts that scenario—of people hurriedly walking past. Although the main subjects take up only a small proportion of the frame, the attention is firmly on them. The people walking passed have been used to frame the scene.

PERSPECTIVES & ANGLES

Creating a good image is not just about having the subject in the right place. Think about where you should be placing yourself too.

As a street photographer, you should be lithe, weaving among the subjects to capture the moment at its greatest impact. This means you must learn to be agile and think outside of the box. Stoop down low, and stand up high for new perspectives. Use your body, and not just your camera.

Behind the subject—less is more

The most obvious perspective of capturing an image would be to stand in front of the subject, however, you can create a sense of mystery by keeping behind, even if this means you cannot see what one might consider important factors, such as a person's face. This further contributes to the ambience of the scene, and can add an intriguing and mystical quality.

↗ **Man Reading Paper—Mumbai, India**
Canon EOS 350D, 24–70mm *f*/2.8 lens
Even though we can't see this man's face, I could tell he was immersed in his newspaper, reading intently.

→ **Woman with Dog—Zurich, Switzerland**
Nikon F3, 50mm *f*/1.8 lens, Kodak 400 film
This well-dressed woman in heels stood out to me, and as I captured the scene it occurred to me that even in photography, less is sometimes more.

Eye level with the subject

Stoop to the eye level of the subject to create a sense of being closer to them. This will produce a feeling of intimacy and will, in most cases, have a positive impact on the image.

Above the subject

Shooting from above can add originality, turning something that might be ordinary into something visually attractive.

↓ Marathon—London, UK
Canon EOS 350D, 18–55mm ƒ/3.5–5.6 lens

At the London Marathon all I saw were people running in a line. With nothing very captivating or engaging to shoot, I walked up on a bridge and looked down. Again, there was nothing particularly picture-worthy until a man began stretching against the wall. Suddenly, the scene had appeal. It was a moment that lasted just a second or two.

↑ Path to the Haji Ali— Mumbai, India
Nikon F3, 50mm ƒ/1.8 lens, Kodak ColorPlus 200 film
Kneeling shifted perspective here.

↓ Sleeping Man—Mumbai, India
Canon EOS 350D, 24–70mm f/2.8 lens
This man slept precariously on a wall, and I sat on the wall behind him to shoot this.

LANDSCAPE OR PORTRAIT?

Choosing whether to capture your scene vertically or horizontally is a decision you should make based on composition, juxtaposition, and how you wish the elements within the frame to be represented.

In the examples shown here of the Golden Temple I shot the same scene both vertically and horizontally as I couldn't immediately decide which would be the better option. As the subject was still I had the time to do this, but this wouldn't always be the case, so you would need to visualize the scene before clicking. Often photography is about visualizing before making your frame. It's important to be able to picture in your mind how you wish a scene to look. This will help you decide how best to shoot it.

→↗ **Golden Temple—Amritsar, India**
Canon EOS 350D, 18–55mm ƒ/3.5–5.6 lens
The Golden Temple is a popular tourist attraction in India, and you tend not to associate the homeless with such a vision, which prompted me to shoot this.

I prefer the landscape version as it captures more of the scenery both behind the homeless man, as well as the pigeons in the foreground, creating more atmosphere.

→ **Boy of Dharavi—Mumbai, India**
Canon EOS 350D, 18–55mm ƒ/3.5–5.6 lens
An example where a vertical frame works, capturing the entire poise of the subject.

THE TECHNICAL

Aperture + Shutter Speed + Light = Exposure

In order to produce captivating photographs in any genre you need to understand a few basic technical aspects. Once you have grasped the concepts of exposure, aperture, and shutter speed you'll be able to use your camera to its maximum potential.

The first element to grasp is that the aperture and shutter speed work in conjunction with one another to set an image's exposure, and the crucial element to all of this is light. The amount of light entering the lens of a camera in many ways defines how an image will look aesthetically. Although you can control how much light strikes the sensor or film for how long—which determines how bright, dark, clear, blurry or sharp your photo is—you still have to work with the available amount of light in the first place.

Aperture explained

The aperture is the hole or diaphragm in a lens through which light travels before reaching the film or the camera's sensor. Controlling the size of aperture controls the amount of light entering the camera.

Aperture is defined by an f/number (or f/stop). This is the ratio of the focal length to the aperture's diameter. Essentially each f/stop represents a quantity of light that passes through the lens. A lower f/number (such as f/2) denotes a large aperture opening that allows more light into the lens, while a larger f/number (such as f/16) denotes a smaller aperture opening, allowing less light into the lens.

Aperture range

Depending on the lens you are using, the range can be as varied as f/2.8 to f/22.

How do I know what aperture to set?

As a rule of thumb:
- Low light—larger aperture (smaller f/number).
- Bright light—smaller aperture (large f/number).
- In low-light situations such as at night, a lower f/number such as f/1.8 is ideal as the aperture of the lens is bigger, allowing as much light in as possible. In bright situations, a smaller aperture (large f/number) is more appropriate as a small amount of bright light will be sufficient to obtain a good exposure. If you use a larger aperture in bright daylight, depending on the shutter speed, your image may be overexposed. The aperture setting should therefore be changed depending on how much light is available.

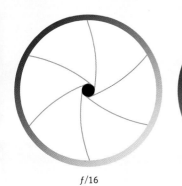

f/16

f/11

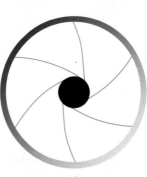

f/8

f/5.6

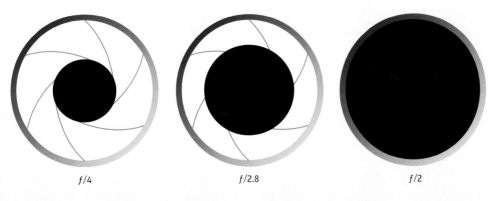

f/4

f/2.8

f/2

You can control the aperture of a camera by changing the *f*/number. A small *f*/number, such as *f*/2, describes a large aperture, while a large *f*/number, such as *f*/16 denotes a small aperture.

DEPTH OF FIELD

As well as governing how much light strikes the film or sensor, the size of the aperture also determines depth of field. Depth of field (DOF) essentially describes the distance range from the camera at which objects will appear in focus.

Controlling depth of field is an essential creative component of photography. In simple terms, setting the DOF allows you to determine how much of the image appears in focus and how much appears blurred.

Large or wide DOF

If you want many or all of the elements within a frame to be in focus, a large DOF is necessary. Even with the focus set at a particular distance from the camera, a large DOF will ensure that many of the other elements both in front of and behind the plane of focus are also sharp.

• Large f/number (small aperture) = large DOF

When to use a large DOF

When all the factors within an image play a central role to the frame itself, and you therefore want most elements or everything to be in focus.

↑ **Selling Tissues—Ankara, Turkey**
Leica M6, 34mm f/1.4 lens, Kodak Ultramax 400 film
An f/number of f/11 was used here, ensuring everything within the frame is in focus.

Small, narrow or shallow DOF

When you set a shallow DOF, the zone of sharpness is very narrow. Objects on the focal plane will be sharp, but all other elements behind or in front of the focal plane will be blurred. Objects become increasingly blurred the greater they are from the focal plane.

• Small f/number (large aperture) = shallow DOF

↑ Carnival Del Pueblo—London, UK
Canon EOS 350D, 50mm f/1.8 lens
In this example I chose an f/number of f/1.8 to isolate one of the women
from the others, as I wanted the focus to be solely on her.

↑ The Office—London, UK
Leica M9, 35mm f/1 lens
f/1 was used here to capture a colleague focused deeply on her computer
screen. I used this very shallow DOF to ensure that nothing but the subject's
face would be in focus, so drawing the viewer's attention to the main subject.

When to use a shallow DOF

- If you wish to isolate the primary subject from the
  foreground or background (also known as selective focus).
- A shallow DOF ensures that potentially distracting
  elements are eliminated.
- To create a more atmospheric image with an emphasis on
  one or a few elements rather than everything.

It is crucial to get the focus exactly spot-on when
using a very shallow DOF. If your main subject is out of focus
your entire image will be ruined. The lower the f/number
you are using, the more obvious any focusing mistakes will
be. To simplify the correlation between aperture and DOF,
remember the following:

- Large f/number = large DOF
- Small f/number = shallow DOF

SHUTTER SPEED

The second factor governing exposure is shutter speed. While the aperture determines how much light enters the camera, the shutter speed determines the length of time the film or sensor is exposed to the light. The brighter the light, the shorter the shutter speed required for an accurate exposure, while if light levels are low the shutter needs to remain open for longer.

A fast shutter speed tends to "freeze" movement in an image and produce a very sharp image. If the shutter speed is slower, movement may appear blurred. While in most cases you're unlikely to want elements in the image to appear blurred, photographers often deliberately use a slower shutter speed to introduce blur for specific effects.

↑ **The World Goes By—Mumbai, India**
Canon EOS 350D, 18–55mm ƒ/3.5–5.6 lens
Here a shutter speed of 1/30 second was used to capture the feeling of movement in the bus. 1/30 second was ideal for the blur due to the brightness of the light. Had it been darker, a slower shutter speed would have been necessary. The subject on the floor was not affected as he was stationary and I held the camera as still as possible.

EXPOSURE

Exposure is a combination of the aperture and shutter speed. To produce the correct exposure, you need to ensure the shutter speed and aperture combination is set appropriately based on the amount of light available.

One of the key creative aspects of photography involves experimenting with the various shutter speed/aperture combinations available to you given the available light. If you increase the shutter speed (to freeze the action, for example), the aperture will need to be larger, resulting in narrower depth of field. Decreasing the shutter speed will have the opposite effect.

In average daylight conditions, there's usually enough (but not too much) light to be able to experiment with the exposure so that you can either have shallow or wide depth of field, or a shutter speed that either freezes or allows action to blur.

However, when light levels are much brighter or darker than average, the scope for experimentation is reduced. In very bright conditions, for example, you may have to have both a fast shutter speed and a narrow aperture to prevent overexposure. These settings won't allow for shallow depth of field for selective focus or creative blur. Obversely, if light levels are very low (to ensure sufficient light reaches the sensor or film) you may have to have both a slow shutter speed and a wide aperture.

↓ **Street Vendor—Istanbul, Turkey**
Leica M6, 35mm f/1.4 lens, Kodak ColorPlus 200 film
In this example I was shooting in sunshine and I used f/1.8, but the shutter speed was too slow, meaning more light than necessary was entering the lens, producing a completely overexposed image. I would either have had to make the f/number larger or increase the shutter speed. I shot this using a manual Leica M6 and while this camera has a light meter to indicate whether the exposure is correct or not, I managed to ignore it due to the lack of time.

In this case you may not be able to freeze fast-moving action or ensure everything in the frame from foreground to background is in focus.

Camera settings

Most cameras today have a fully automatic setting that will set the exposure for you based on the light level. However, using the Auto setting means you can't control depth of field or shutter speed. Instead try using one of the semi-manual settings, such as Aperture Priority. In this mode you set the aperture (to control DOF), and the camera determines the right shutter speed for a correct exposure. This is the mode I use most frequently when shooting with my DSLR.

Alternatively, in Shutter Priority you set the shutter speed and the camera sets the aperture; while in Manual mode you set both the shutter speed and the aperture—this setting gives you ultimate creative control, but requires practice and experience before it becomes second nature.

Most fully manual cameras have an in-built light meter that assists you when manually setting the aperture and shutter speed. The light meter indicates when the exposure is correct within the viewfinder of the camera.

← **Tailor—Ankara, Turkey**
Leica M6, 35mm ƒ/1.4 lens, Kodak Ultramax 400 film
Here is an illustration of good exposure, where the shopkeeper's face is clearly visible through the reflection of the glass.

SHOOTING AT NIGHT

There is a plethora of activity going on outside at night, but don't let the lack of light hinder your ability to shoot in darker scenarios.

Flash or no flash?

There are no set rules about using flash on your camera, however, a camera's flash will not only draw attention to you, but will be even more obtrusive for the subject at night. Imagine walking down the street at night to find someone pointing their camera at you, but then additionally having a beam of light strike your face. It could be intimidating and indeed scary for the subject, so it is best avoided. Aesthetically you may also lose the natural quality of an image by using flash. For that reason the following tips are designed for shooting in low light without the use of flash. You will need to bear some factors in mind when shooting at night without a flash:

← **Silhouette in the Sky— Mumbai, India**
Nikon F3, 50mm ƒ/1.8 lens, Kodak ColorPlus 200 film
I looked up here to see a boy waving at me. The direction and lack of light meant that he would be obscured as a silhouette, but I liked how this contrasted with the blue of the sky, even if none of his features are clear. Use any available light sources to your advantage.

- Use a "fast" lens. A fast lens refers to one that has a large aperture such as f/1.8. Such lenses allow more light inside, ideal for low-light scenes. A lens such as a 50mm f/1.8 is not only cheap, but is also a fast prime lens making shooting at night much more viable. The lower the f/stop you use, the better your night shots will be. Unless you are looking to create a funky or blurry effect, you will want a fast lens to "freeze" the scene under low-light circumstances.
- Use a fast film or high ISO. In film photography, the ISO refers to the light sensitivity of the film, and is measured in numbers, for example, ISO 100, 200, 400, 800, 1600. If you have ever used film you will have noticed that you can buy them with various ISOs, such as Kodak 400. The higher the number, the more sensitive the film is to light.

    In digital photography ISO refers to the light sensitivity of the image sensor, and is measured in a similar way to that of film. Using a high ISO (such as 800 or 1600) is recommended in low-light situations as it increases the sensor's light sensitivity therefore allowing faster shutter speeds to prevent motion blur. The downside to using a high ISO is that the images will be grainier or "noisier." I say "downside," but this is not necessarily a bad thing with film. Grain can add an authentic quality to an image, as well as create an atmospheric and natural look—although this is less true of digital noise, which is usually ugly and undesirable.
- Keep as still as possible. If you are shooting in broad daylight, motion blur is usually not an issue as there is

↑ **Balloon Man—Mumbai, India**
Canon EOS 350D, 18–55mm f/3.5–5.6 lens
Most compact cameras have a night-time function that typically adjusts all the settings to better suit low-light scenes. The following tips are designed to help you make the most of shooting at night or where there is a distinct lack of light, in order to create effective images.

enough light to create sharp images. However, at night where there is a lack of light, blurry images are very common, and even tiny movements of the camera can cause blurry pictures, even if you are using the fastest lens, fastest shutter speed, and highest ISO that your camera will allow.

One way of getting passed motion blur is by holding your camera as still as possible, but also choosing subjects that are still, for example, people waiting for a bus or train.

↑ A Face in the Darkness—Istanbul, Turkey
Canon EOS 350D, 50mm *f*/1.8 lens
A man's face is lit up in the darkness just as he looked
into the lens of my camera.

- Read the light. It is necessary to be able to use any
  available light sources to your advantage when
  shooting in low light. After all, it is the amount of light
  that will determine just how your image will turn out in
  terms of clarity. If there is a light source available, try
  to capture your subject at an angle that the light will hit
  at its most effective.

↓ Hope—Mumbai, India
This image was captured outside Mahim Station in Mumbai, the
target of a terrorist bombing a few weeks before, killing scores of
people. I used a compact digital (HP Photosmart R707) with the
flash turned off to capture this woman walking in front of a large
billboard displaying the word "Hope." The road is a busy one with
constant traffic, which is reflected by the heavy light streaks. The
blur for me added a surreal and dreamy quality to a scene that was
meaningful and symbolic. This is an example of using
imperfections to your advantage.

- Experiment with your camera settings. On New Year's Eve in London I wanted to capture the fireworks from the London Eye, behind a clock striking midnight. The only lens I had on me allowed an f/number of f/3.5, which isn't particularly fast in a very low-light situation. I therefore upped the ISO to the highest possible that the camera would allow, which was 1600 (many other DSLRs allow for higher ISOs).

  Before midnight I tested different settings to see what could be attained.

↖ f/3.5
ISO 1600, shutter speed 1/60 seconds
Now the exposure is on the clock face so that the time is visible, but also the London Eye is clear and sharp.

← f/3.5
ISO 1600, shutter speed 1/4 seconds
The shutter speed is far too slow, creating blown-out areas and no clarity.

→ f/5.6
ISO 1600, shutter speed 1/60 seconds
I kept the same settings when the clock struck midnight, capturing the fireworks from the London Eye as well as the time. Preparation can pay off.

TIP
To hold your camera as still as possible, push your arms against your chest for added support.

TIPS & TRICKS

Being inconspicuous is a major advantage when it comes to street photography. How is it possible to create a good picture without being intrusive, and capture moments without being noticed?

There are a number of ways to blend into the crowd and be "invisible;" and while it is not always necessary, it can certainly help, particularly in areas where there are not many tourists, or where people walking around with cameras is an uncommon sight.

Dress

Don't wear clothes that make you stand out from the crowd. If abroad, wear local clothing, particularly if you are in a region that is very different from your usual surroundings, and where you may receive unwanted stares by wearing what you would normally wear at home.

Don't keep lots of cameras around your neck when shooting. In my experience, looking like a tourist makes you seem like a novice and a happy snapper, which tends not to draw looks. In short, try not to look like a pro!

← Reading the Paper—Istanbul, Turkey
Canon EOS 350D, 18–55mm *f*/3.5–5.6 lens
I shot this man reading his paper very quickly, barely pausing in front of him.

Noise

Generally, being noisy is a sure way to attract attention, but sometimes this can have its advantages. If shooting in a quiet museum or library for example, the sound of a camera shutter will most likely attract attention, but simple things such as coughing while clicking can drown out the sound of a camera. It might sound silly, but this kind of tactic has been used in museums by legendary street photographer Elliott Erwitt and has proved to be effective.

Choice of camera

Using a camera with a quiet shutter can make a significant difference to your ability to go unnoticed. Most DSLRs, for example, have loud shutters and in quiet surroundings will be highly audible. Rangefinders are the top choice for many street photographers as the sound of the shutter is incredibly quiet, making shooting inconspicuously a lot easier.

People on the street generally take rangefinders, compact digitals and mobile phone cameras less seriously than SLRs as they are smaller and quieter, therefore giving the impression that you are not a "serious" photographer.

← **Saatchi Gallery—London, UK**
Canon EOS 350D, 18–55mm *f*/3.5–5.6 lens
Although I used a DSLR here, which has a fairly loud shutter sound, the subjects were quite far away and deep in conversation, so didn't notice me.

Walking around with a large lens on an SLR instantly makes you look like a professional, and people find such cameras a lot more intimidating. Perception counts for a lot.

If you are using a mobile phone or compact digital camera, turn all sounds off. It sounds obvious but it's an easy mistake to make!

It is possible to give the impression that you are not making a photo at all, simply by positioning the camera in a way that looks like you are not actually looking through the viewfinder. This method is known as "shooting from the hip" or shooting "blindly."

Shooting from the hip

Shooting from the hip is a valuable skill that all street photographers should develop. It enables you to capture scenes without actually looking through the viewfinder, thus giving the impression you aren't actually using the camera at all. The technique also allows you to be inventive with angles and different perspectives, without anyone noticing you're actually photographing.

Whatever camera you are using, you will need a sense of perspective when shooting blindly. You will also need to know where to hold the camera in order to ensure the lens is facing toward the subject and is not too high up, low down or

← Quadruplets—Istanbul, Turkey
Leica M6, 35mm ƒ/1.4 lens, Kodak Ultramax 400 film
Using a rangefinder allowed me to shoot from the hip easily, with the subjects here barely taking any notice of me. The shutter sound is so quiet it is inaudible in a busy street.

↗ Chatting Up—Istanbul, Turkey
Leica M6, 35mm ƒ/1.4 lens, Kodak Ultramax 400 film
Again, a rangefinder here, although aimed at the subject, was barely noticed by him, and if he did, he didn't object to being photographed, most likely because he didn't hear the shutter click. A loud shutter noise can be intimidating for many if shooting in close proximity.

pointing off to the left or right. This takes practice—be prepared to get it wrong the first few times. Be patient and persistent as this is a skill that will most certainly pay off when shooting street photography.

Focusing, exposing, and composing

- **Auto settings**

  To help focus, if you are using a camera that has an autofocus function such as a DSLR or compact digital camera, as long as you are aiming your camera correctly and it is positioned well, the focus will be correct.

- **Manual settings**

  If you are using a fully manual camera, such as a film rangefinder, shooting from the hip is not as simple as pointing and shooting. In this case you will need to focus and expose correctly without actually looking through the viewfinder.

  How will you do this? Most film SLRs and rangefinders have distance indicators on top of the focus ring in both feet and meters. To use this successfully, you will need to judge how far your subject is from the camera, and then turn the focus ring to point to the correct distance.

TIP:

If you are shooting from the hip and with a manual camera, it's quite a feat to get every setting correct in a split second. To help you, if you use a large f/number more of the image will be in focus, so even if your focus is incorrect, it won't show in the image. You should also check the settings beforehand so that you have the exposure set correctly before you begin shooting.

EXERCISE:

Wherever you are, even in your bedroom, pick various objects and guess their position without looking through the viewfinder. Take a shot and see how much of the object you managed to capture. Over time your judgment of where the camera is pointing will become more accurate until it becomes second nature.

CULTURAL SENSITIVITIES

When you are out and about in public, be sensitive to your surroundings and act accordingly. For example, in a library you are unlikely to see people shouting or running. We all adapt and amend our behavior according to where we are—and the same applies to a street photographer.

Let's consider two contrasting cities. I have spent a significant amount of time shooting both in London and Mumbai, and these two cities vary greatly in terms of culture. This in turn affects the way I shoot when I am out on the street of these two diverse places.

Londoners are used to keeping to themselves on public transport and in general being unobtrusive goes without saying. Getting too close to someone or staring, for example, is considered rude and not in line with cultural expectations. Furthermore, it is almost as though there is stigma associated with taking photos of strangers. For this reason, my natural instinct is to be cautious of what people could perceive as unacceptable behavior.

Mumbai is a heavily populated city with noise, bustle, and general activity on every street corner. The sensory overload is at times so overwhelming that I struggle to decide what to capture. As a result, the sense of personal space becomes much smaller. There is no choice in the matter. You are often walking on streets so crowded that physically bumping into people is common. People are more

↑ **Mumbai Railways—Mumbai, India**
Nikon F3, 50mm ƒ/1.8, Kodak Ultramax 400 film
In Mumbai walking along railway tracks is a common everyday occurrence, and there are often no doors on the trains, with commuters hanging out of the trains as they travel. This man stared right at me without reacting in any way. He kept the same expression he had before he spotted me. This is commonplace. In this rather risky shot I held onto a pole while I stuck my head out of the doorway, having to manually focus as I was using a Nikon F3 camera, which does not have an auto-focus functionality, all the while trying not to fall out.

It took me at least a few seconds to capture this moment—much longer than usual. While I wouldn't recommend risking your life to capture such a scene, it was possible as it is nothing unusual in Mumbai, and yet, in London this kind of scenario would not arise. I took advantage of the situation to create an image I would not ordinarily produce.

curious and inquisitive, and in my experience do not become hostile even if a camera is pointing directly at them. On the whole, it is viable to openly shoot without negative repercussions.

← Bike Lady—Mumbai, India
Canon EOS 350D, 18–55mm
ƒ/3.5–5.6 lens
If I attempted to sit on the back of a motorbike without a helmet in London, there would be a good chance of being arrested. The cultural differences and lax rules and regulations in India made this shot possible. I was simply capturing this very essence in this shot—a woman perched precariously on the back of a bike, holding onto her handbag.

← Cricket Boys—Mumbai, India
Canon EOS 350D, 18–55mm ƒ/3.5–5.6 lens
Here a group of boys were playing cricket as I walked passed with my camera. I snapped a couple of candid images before they all ran toward me and spontaneously posed. I found it to be a wonderful moment as it captured the innocent essence of children playing a sport that in this country is followed by almost everyone.

Children

There is a general sensitivity that exists around photographing children in the UK. A paranoid society has made it unacceptable. I have previously asked for permission from parents to capture their children on camera, and been told "no." Although frustrating this is understandable and I always respect parents' wishes.

In Mumbai, things work a little differently. Children absolutely love the camera and almost fight to be in the frame.

What is most important is that you show respect at all times, irrespective of cultural differences. If a subject is not comfortable with being photographed it will show.

Before traveling to another country read up on the culture and how this could affect your ability to shoot. Adapt to local customs to ensure that you won't end up upsetting anyone. It always helps to know what the local laws are and whether photography could be affected.

STREET PHOTOGRAPHY & THE LAW

When shooting in the public domain, it is useful to know what your rights are, and what you can and can't do in terms of the local laws, as these could very well affect your ability to take photos.

Particularly in the wake of terrorist events there has been a wave of paranoia among the general public, and perfectly innocent photographers are being stopped and questioned by the police, simply for snapping away in the street. Do not let this intimidate you. Photographing in the street has certainly become a contentious issue, but remember, in most cases you have the right to be out and about with your camera.

Kishan Chandarana is a London-based lawyer, whose own brushes with the authorities while taking photographs of the Kremlin caused him to look at the laws and practices around taking photographs in urban settings.

← **Police Surveillance—London, UK**
Canon EOS 350D, 18–55mm *f*/3.5–5.6 lens
A policeman in London filming protesters during a large rally.

The law is subject to change and the information below may not be current at the time of print. This section of the book is for reference purposes only and does not constitute legal advice.

Myths and truths—UK

Almost every street photographer, from the amateur to the most serious professional will regale you with tales of being stopped and questioned by the police or private security guards. While law and practice are much less clearly defined in certain countries (as I found out in Russia), in the UK, there is specific guidance on photography in public places.

Misunderstanding of anti-terrorism legislation is frequently cited as an excuse to stop street photographers from plying their craft. The latest guidance from the Metropolitan Police states:

"Officers have the power to view digital images contained in mobile telephones or cameras carried by a person searched under S43 of the Terrorism Act 2000, to discover whether the images constitute evidence that the person is involved in terrorism. Officers also have the power to seize and retain any article found during the search which the officer reasonably suspects may constitute evidence that the person is a terrorist. This includes any mobile telephone or camera containing such evidence."

The guidance goes onto state that officers do not have the power to delete digital images or destroy film at any point during a search. The deletion or destruction of a digital image can only take place if it is lawfully sanctioned by a Court Order.

The terrorism legislation also restricts publishing or communicating information about members of the (i) armed forces; (ii) intelligence services; or (iii) the police, where the information is designed to provide practical assistance to a person committing or preparing an act of terrorism. This is especially noteworthy for photographers who publish their photographs on social media websites.

→ **Myths & Truths—UK & USA**
Some common misconceptions and the truth behind the myths.

MYTHS & TRUTHS IN THE UK AND THE USA

MYTH: Street photography is illegal:

TRUTH: UK
While there are certain restrictions around photographs on private property, there are no restrictions on taking photographs on public land.

TRUTH: USA
While there are certain restrictions around photographs on private property, there are no restrictions on taking photographs on public land. Notably, the definition of a public place is much narrower in the US than in the UK. This means places such as parks and museums may still fall under the definition of private property.

MYTH: You need permission to photograph buildings on public land:

TRUTH: UK
With the exception of Trafalgar Square and Parliament Square in London and any Royal Park, there is no general requirement to seek permission to photograph on public land.

TRUTH: USA
While there is no general requirement to seek permission to photograph on public land, the definition of public land is narrower than one would expect. There are also restrictions on photographing military/naval installations or equipment.

MYTH: You can't photograph buildings on private property:

TRUTH: UK
There is nothing to prohibit photography of buildings on private property if the photographs are being taken from public land. Photographs of private property, taken on private property, can be taken if permission has been sought from the owner of private property.

TRUTH: USA
There is nothing to prohibit photography of buildings on private property if the photographs are being taken from public land. Photographs of private property, taken on private property, can be taken if permission has been sought from the owner of private property.

MYTH: "I am a police officer/traffic warden/security guard and I can delete/destroy your photos:"

TRUTH: UK
Although a police officer may prevent you from taking pictures in certain limited circumstances, no police officer, traffic warden or security guard can make you delete a photograph.

TRUTH: USA
Police officers may prevent you from taking pictures in certain limited circumstances by closing off access to certain areas. Moreover, police officers are able to view photographs on a camera. No police officer or private security guard can make you delete a photograph.

MYTH: Taking a person's photograph is a breach of their civil rights:

TRUTH: UK
While invading someone's personal space and obstruction their passage down a street may constitute harassment, there is nothing to prevent you from taking a photograph of another individual. Moreover, the person photographed does not have the right to make you delete your photographs.

TRUTH: USA
While harassing an individual and obstructing their passage down a street may constitute harassment, there is nothing to prevent you from taking a photograph of another individual in a public place, unless the individual has a "reasonable expectation of privacy" (for example, in a hotel room).

Myths and truths—USA

In the USA there are many myths around the powers of the authorities to prohibit photography and interrogate individuals in the interest of national security. The reality is that the restrictions on street photography are somewhat limited, though the police have other powers with respect to trespass, harassment, and obstruction of public passage.

The main considerations in the USA are less around laws impacting photography and more around individuals or the owners of private property enforcing their rights. The USA, being a more litigious environment, requires a photographer to take care over how a photograph represents (or misrepresents) an individual or private property.

Photographers should also be sensitive to state laws, which impose state-wide restrictions on photography. Federal laws, overlaid by state laws should then be considered in the context of other regulations from government bodies. For example, the Transportation Security Administration (TSA) imposes restrictions on what can be photographed as people are being security screened at airports, despite the airport being (in some cases) a public place.

Copyright, ownership, and distribution—UK and USA

Photographs are classified as "artistic works" and in the UK and USA the owner of the copyright in a photograph is the photographer, as the creator of the artistic work. While copyright might subsist in certain photographs, enforcing rights to a photograph is notoriously difficult. The advent of social networking websites has also blurred the exact ownership of certain photographs. This is because the terms and conditions of certain social networking websites require that ownership rights in photographs are assigned to the social network. Moreover, certain social networking websites require confirmation that any photograph uploaded is actually owned by the person uploading the photograph.

UK—In the UK, copyright in a photograph continues for 70 years from the end of the year in which a photographer dies. The owner of a photograph has the exclusive right to copy the photograph. Copying of a photograph or any substantial part of a photograph by any other person would be an infringement of another photographer's copyright. This should not be confused with copying the subject matter of a picture, which would not be a breach of another person's copyright.

USA—In the USA, it is possible to register your copyright with the US Copyright Office, provided this is done within a certain period of the photograph being published. The photograph must be sufficiently "original" to be registered. Apart from registering the photograph, it is also advisable that the copyright symbol "©" be placed on or by photographs along with: (i) the date (or at least the year of publication); and (ii) the name of the individual (individual's company) that owns the photograph. Where a photograph is transferred for advertising, trade or any other commercial purpose, a release form is required. Given the litigious nature of the USA, the transferee of the photograph may also ask for proof that the transferrer had the necessary permissions to photograph on private land.

Making a photographer's life easier

When dealing with the authorities in the UK, remember that they may not be entirely aware of the law around photography on public land. Outside of the UK, be aware that there may be local laws and practices that prohibit photography. Above all, be safe, and consider using the tactics below to achieve the photographs that you want.

1) Be polite to members of the public, security guards, and police.
2) Do not take risks to protect your equipment—your personal safety should be the main priority.
3) Although asking for permission may not be necessary, it can be helpful if you want to include people in the image. You may find that the people you ask can show you other areas of photographic interest.
4) You may find in certain countries that payment is requested to take certain photographs. Refusal or non cooperation with local customs may lead to violent or unpleasant behavior.
5) If approached by police, do not quote the law, chapter and verse. Be polite and cooperate by explaining your interest in street photography. In the UK, if a police officer does not act with honesty, integrity, and respect, a complaint against the officer can be submitted to the Independent Police Complaints Commission (IPCC).
6) If you would like to take photographs on private property, remember to seek the permission of the owner. Permission in writing, which defines the exact location in which permission is granted, is best. This is useful in the event that there is a later dispute about whether or not permission is granted.
7) Check the terms and conditions of any social media website that you upload photographs onto. If you intend to derive monetary benefit from a photograph, do not accidentally give away ownership of a photograph.

4. EQUIPMENT

It's not what you own, but how you use what you have.

THE CAMERA

Your camera should feel like an extension of your body. You shouldn't be constrained and restricted by your camera—instead it should feel entirely natural.

The all-important question that any photographer needs to consider is "what kit goes in the bag?"

With any type of photography, equipment plays an integral role in the photographer's ability to create outstanding shots.

Does size really matter?

The equipment you carry with you will affect your ability to shoot successfully and with ease. For example, if you are carrying around a large, heavy camera with a telephoto lens on a tripod, you will not only draw unnecessary attention to yourself, but it will also slow you down and affect your mobility.

Bearing this in mind, you should ask yourself the following questions:

- How easy will it be for me to carry the camera around?
- Do I want to shoot film or digital?
- Do I want to shoot manual or auto? Or perhaps semi-auto such as Aperture or Shutter Priority on DSLRs.
- What is my budget?

Using film has running costs associated with it. It is also worth noting that expensive equipment does not automatically guarantee fantastic images if you don't know how to use it!

← **Camera Shop—Tel Aviv, Israel**
Canon EOS 350D, 18–55mm f/3.5–5.6 lens
One of the first cameras I used was my mother's Nikon EM (a film SLR) made in the late 1970s. I was used to shooting with automatic settings on a digital camera, and I had initially dismissed this as an old useless box, until I put a roll of film into it. I was amazed at the results. Don't underestimate the potential of older cameras—they can be reliable and sturdy, and shouldn't be discounted. In fact, many street photographers only swear by such "old-school" equipment for their reputation in creating terrific images.

In this chapter we'll look at the various types of equipment a street photographer may consider using, and help you assess the merits of these. Do you really need that exorbitantly expensive digital rangefinder, or would you get more enjoyment from a plastic film camera?

Looking closer to home

Before you consider buying anything, however, look at what you already have access to. Can you borrow anyone's cameras? Clean out the attic and ask your parents or relatives what they have boxed away. You might be surprised! Charity shops, eBay, and second-hand camera stores are also great places to pick up a bargain.

↓ Camera—Nikon EM with a 50mm ƒ/1.8 lens
Manufactured: 1979–1984
Type: 35mm film
Cost: Available second-hand for around $150.

↗ NY Parade—London, UK
Nikon EM, 50mm ƒ/1.8 lens,
Ilford XP2 Super 400 film
The Nikon EM is a very basic and relatively lightweight film SLR.

→ Jumble Sale—London, UK
Nikon EM, 50mm ƒ/1.8 lens,
Kodak Gold 200 film
Here I was captivated by the multitude of colors, and shooting with film can really accentuate tones, depending on the type of film used.

THE BARE ESSENTIALS

Carry only the essentials. Don't be constrained by carrying too much equipment or feel restricted by too little. Work with what you have. A bag full of equipment may give you more options, but it will also stop you from shooting with complete freedom as you start wondering whether to change cameras or swap lenses.

Since street photography is considered a way of life, the only way to avoid missing a moment is by carrying your camera at all times. Ideally therefore, you want your equipment to have the following properties:

- Small and light enough to fit into a shoulder bag or small rucksack—carrying it shouldn't be a burden or make you look intimidating.
- Something you can keep around your neck, over your shoulder or in your hand that won't affect your ability to carry out your other daily tasks—for example, if you're out shopping, you want to be able to continue shopping without your camera constantly getting in the way or becoming so heavy that you decide not to take it out with you.
- Comfortable to use. If you're awkwardly having to fiddle with a twisted strap or your camera keeps bumping into things, this will only make the street shooting experience frustrating for you.

Over the next few pages, we'll look at the pros and cons of some of the more popular types of camera.

THE RANGEFINDER

The rangefinder camera is considered to be the best all-round camera for street photography. Rangefinders utilize a distance-determining mechanism known as a rangefinder (hence the name). Looking through the rangefinder shows two identical images of the scene. Using a control wheel, the photographer adjusts one image so that it is superimposed exactly over the second, indicating the point of focus. The rangefinder device is linked to the focusing mechanism and in this way the lens is brought into focus.

A notable feature of rangefinders is that when you look through the viewfinder you are looking straight out onto the scene, as opposed to with an SLR where you are looking into the camera, via a prism and a moving mirror, and then out

through the lens. With rangefinders, there's no moving mirror. You focus and compose through a window at the top of the camera. The lack of a moving mirror, which makes that familiar KER-KLACK noise common to SLRs, ensures that rangefinders are significantly quieter to use—a highly attractive feature for street photographers.

Leica rangefinders were used by early esteemed street photographers like Cartier-Bresson, and to this day they remain a highly reputable and popular camera choice among street shooters.

While many rangefinders are now discontinued, new Leicas are available for purchase including digital rangefinders, such as the M8 and M9 models. However, at around $8,000, a brand new digital Leica is not cheap!

← **Camera—Leica M6 with a 35mm *f*/1.4 lens**
Manufactured: 1984–1998
Type: 35mm film
Cost: $2700 bought second-hand

Why a rangefinder?

What makes a camera like this so desirable for street photography?

- **Quiet operation**
  Rangefinders are extremely quiet as there is no internal moving mirror. This makes the shutter noise barely audible in many situations, allowing photographers to get closer to their subjects without being noticed.

- **Small, compact, and relatively lightweight**
  Rangefinders are compact—you can easily carry one around without being weighed down. Rangefinder lenses are also small in comparison to the equivalent focal-length SLR lenses.

- **No momentary viewfinder black-out**
  When the mirror in an SLR moves up during capture, you cannot see through the viewfinder until the capture is complete and the mirror is back in position. Because a viewfinder on a rangefinder does not go through the lens, you can watch the scene continue to evolve as you take the photo, and better prepare for a second shot.

- **Wide field of view**
  Rangefinder viewfinders usually have a larger field of view than the lens being used, allowing photographers to see what is happening outside of the frame lines. This is useful when predicting the behavior of subjects, or to see people moving into the frame before they do so.

- **Shoot with both eyes open**
The design of most rangefinders allows photographers to use their right eye to look through the viewfinder instead of the usual left eye, and to keep both eyes open when shooting. This is advantageous if you want to be able to see what else is happening around the subject, again useful when predicting a shot. Keeping both eyes open can also have tactical advantages as you can be seen to be looking at something completely different while shooting, thus giving the impression to the subject that you are not photographing them at all. If you're only used to using your left eye, this method of shooting can take some getting used to.

- **Interchangeable lenses**
Like SLRs, rangefinders can have interchangeable lenses although the range of available lenses is much less varied. This is not necessarily a bad thing and we will look at different lens types later. Some rangefinders have fixed lenses, such as the Olympus 35 series.

- **Easy and accurate focusing in low light**
It is much easier to focus with precision in darker conditions with a rangefinder. Autofocus mechanisms on many DSLRs struggle in poor light.

- **Intimidation factor**
Rangefinders look less intimidating to the general person on the street. To someone uninitiated to the rangefinder, they are less likely to take a defensive stance toward them because they look compact and amateur compared with a professional-looking DSLR. Perception has a big role to play in appearing discreet.

- **No shooting modes**
Modern cameras have a vast range of modes and settings that can be used for night, sports, portraits, macro, face recognition, and even smile detection. Rangefinders don't have these options, so it's down to you to know what settings you need to use in such situations. Rangefinders are not point-and-shoot devices, and learning how to expose and focus is essential with a manual rangefinder. Once you get to grips with it, however, it's a great way to photograph, as anyone who uses one will tell you. As a photographer you are in full control of the camera, and it is highly satisfying knowing an image you have created was down to your technical capabilities as well as your artistry. Many would argue that using a manual camera such as a rangefinder makes you a better photographer.

Purists of street photography use rangefinders as they encompass all the properties of a camera ideal for street shooting. They have a refined elegance and sophistication about them that makes them desirable and the first choice of camera for many.

← 3 Legged Dog & 4 Suits—London, UK
Leica M6, 35mm ƒ/1.4 lens, Lucky 100 film
Although the dog here was on a leash,
I purposely waited and framed the image
without the dog's owner in it, to capture
an unusual moment.

The drawback to rangefinders
The real downside is that rangefinders are not commonly
made today. In the 1950s there were many models to choose
from with varied price ranges, but today the only new models
are eye-wateringly expensive, and even second-hand cameras
made by Leica and compatible lenses cost more than many
people can afford.

However, if you're determined to go via the rangefinder
route there are a number of reputable rangefinder brands aside
from Leica that are more affordable, such as the Voigtlander
Bessa, Konica Hexar, several Olympus models, the Argus
"Brick," and the inexpensive Canon Canonet to name a few.

← Icecream Man—Istanbul, Turkey
Leica M6, 35mm ƒ/1.4 lens, Kodak Gold 400 film
A rangefinder here allowed me to get fairly close to the
subject, and although he was aware of me, he didn't
change his behavior and he even asked me what kind of
camera I was using. The camera here allows this image to
be more than just a holiday snapshot through the use of
film and an aperture of ƒ/1.4.

SLR & DIGITAL SLR CAMERAS

SLR (single lens reflex) camera features a moving mirror system. Light from the scene enters through the lens and is directed via a series of mirrors and a pentaprism out through the viewfinder. So in essence you are looking through the lens (TTL), allowing you to see precisely what will be captured on camera, whether on film or on a memory card via an imaging sensor.

When you press the shutter release to capture an image, the mirror (known as the reflex) flips up out of the way, allowing the light to pass directly through to the film or sensor, capturing exactly what you are seeing via the viewfinder.

Historically film SLRs offered an excellent trade off between image quality, portability, and versatility (thanks to interchangeable lenses), making them the most popular camera type. This popularity has continued into the digital age, and now thanks to their relative affordability, DSLRs are seen in abundance wherever you go.

Advantages:
Durable, reliable, sturdy, and with a wide range available to suit different budgets. A large range of interchangeable lenses make for good versatility. Auto-settings on DSLRs and some film SLRs can make shooting with these cameras simple. It is also possible to shoot in manual mode, providing full control over the camera.

↑ **Camera—Nikon F3**
Manufactured: 1980–2001
Type: Film SLR
Cost: Available second-hand for around $250
My favorite film SLR is the Nikon F3, which is fully manual and has a detachable eye-level pentaprism allowing you to remove it and look down through the camera to compose and focus. Not having to bring the camera to your eye can help when being discreet.

Disadvantages:
Bulky, noisy and heavy (particularly with certain lenses) they are not the most discreet cameras available.

Factors to consider if buying an SLR

· Film or digital?

It may sound like a retrograde step to buy a film SLR when there's such a vast choice of affordable DSLRs now on the market, but many people prefer the look of film, particularly when it comes to street photography. And a little money goes a long way with film cameras. A Canon EOS 3, for example, is available for around $200 second-hand and provides auto and semi-auto settings. So if you don't want to manually focus and expose, but you do want to use film, this is a good, cheap option.

Remember, with film cameras you won't have the luxury of viewing your photos on an LCD screen after taking them.

· Crop factor

The sensors in most DSLRs are smaller than a standard frame of 35mm film. APS-C format sensors, as they are collectively known, vary in size from between 21mm to 29mm along the longest edge, making a full-frame about 1.6 times larger. The smaller sensor effectively reduces the field of view so that a 50mm lens effectively becomes 80mm (50mm x 1.6). This effect is known as the crop factor.

Does the crop factor matter with street photography? Well yes and no. The full potential of the scene that could be captured won't be, unlike a film camera where the entire scene that the lens can capture will be caught on camera. Full-frame DSLRs are available that have no crop factor, but these are costly, so while losing some of the frame isn't ideal, if you can afford to compromise on crop factor it will save you a lot of money. My DSLR has a crop factor, but I don't find it particularly problematic or frustrating. Having said that, it's quite useful and almost liberating to be able to use a full-frame camera such as my Nikon F3 film SLR, knowing that when I use a 50mm lens on it, I am getting what it says on the tin—50mm.

• Maximum ISO

If you intend to be out and about at night, you'll want to consider a camera that has the ability to use high ISO—anything up to 6400, for example—but noise will increase.

• What cameras do your friends own?

Particularly if you're on a budget, borrowing lenses is a great idea. If many people around you have Nikon DSLRs, you may want to go for a Nikon body as well.

• Budget

If you have untold riches, a full-frame DSLR such as the Canon 5D Mk II with a 35mm f/1.4 lens would be great, but this simply isn't realistic for most of us. As new models are released pretty much every year, you can pick up some very good value-for-money used equipment. If you are buying off the internet make sure the camera functions properly, and that you can return it if necessary.

LENSES

SLR cameras are compatible with a wide range of interchangeable lenses, which is handy if you want lenses for different scenarios, from short focal length wide-angle to longer telephoto lenses.

When you buy a DSLR, it typically comes with a kit lens such as an 18–55mm lens. Although they're not necessarily of the highest quality, they provide perfectly acceptable results, and this is what I've used for many years, and continue to use occasionally.

While this kit lens has its advantages and is great to use on a daily basis, with street photography there are a number of lenses considered particularly ideal, and the most significant of these are prime lenses.

→ **Camera—Canon EOS 350D (Rebel XT) with an 18–55mm *f*/3.5–5.6 lens**
Manufactured: 2005–2008
Type: Digital SLR
Cost: Available second-hand for around $350
The 18–55mm lens is light, but not discreet. The maximum aperture is *f*/3.5, which means that it's not the fastest lens either, but I've always found it a great all-round lens for the day, particularly since it's very wide at 18mm.

Prime vs zoom lenses

A prime lens is one with a fixed focal length. Put simply, you cannot zoom in and out.

Typical prime lenses used for street include focal lengths of 50mm, the wider 35mm, and wider still 24mm.

Prime lenses are favorites with many street photographers and here's why:

- **Fast speed = Low-light capability**
  Because they are of a fixed focal length, prime lenses contain fewer elements and moving parts. This means that they tend to have larger apertures, which as we have seen, is advantageous when it comes to shooting in low-light conditions. Prime lenses are available with maximum apertures of 1.2, 1, and even 0.95, unlike zoom lenses for which the maximum aperture is *f*/2.8.

- **Shallow DOF**
  With such a large aperture, prime lenses allow you to use a very shallow DOF should you wish to. So throwing the background way out of focus is easily done with a prime lens.

↑ Last Train Home—Tokyo, Japan

Canon EOS 350D, 50mm f/1.8 lens

Taken with a prime lens, the surroundings are thrown out of focus. This was particularly ideal here where I wanted the focus firmly on the main subject without distractions.

↗ The Streets of the East—London, UK

Canon EOS 350D, 18–55mm f/3.5–5.6 lens

Here, the 18–55mm lens was wide enough to capture both subjects easily.

→ Standing Still—Istanbul, Turkey

Canon EOS 350D, 18–55mm f/3.5–5.6 lens

This lens allowed me to capture the bustle around the main subject and keep everything in focus too.

- **Lightweight**
  As prime lenses are of a fixed focal length, they have fewer parts, and are lighter and easier to carry.

- **Smaller**
  The standard aperture (f/1.8–f/2) 50mm and 35mm lenses are generally quite small and compact, making them appear less intrusive and intimidating. However, super-fast lenses, such as the Canon 35mm f/1.2 L lens, can be physically much larger than standard primes.

- **They make you think**
  Although you can't zoom in and out (which many might see as a disadvantage), prime lenses force the photographer to really think about composition. It encourages photographers to immerse themselves into a scene as a participant and really capture the action as close as possible. This makes for more dramatic and more intense photos. Prime lenses make you think about subject placement and framing, and over time will help to develop perception and awareness. It's more challenging to use a prime lens, but this makes it far more fun and forces you to be creative and inventive.

→ **Same Shit—London, UK**
Canon EOS 350D, 35mm f/2 lens
The 35mm lens is great for portraits. In this case it allowed me to not only capture the subject's serious and determined look, but also his high-impact placard—all without having to get uncomfortably close, or stand too far back to forfeit the expression.

- **Quality**

  As there are less parts and elements between the subject and image sensor, prime lenses tend to produce sharper images with more accurate and vibrant colors than many comparably priced zoom lenses.

- **Cost**

  Prime lenses needn't be expensive. A very popular example is the Canon EF 50mm f/1.8 lens, which is available new for around $100. I bought mine second-hand for $60. It's small, lightweight, but fast and capable of excellent results. However, do bear in mind that with a crop sensor camera the effective focal length is 80mm, which may not be wide enough for many street scenes. The equivalent lens for a cropped sensor camera is a 35mm f/2, which is similar in size, but not as fast and more expensive. The same issues tend to apply to other manufacturers such as Nikon.

  Even wider-angle prime lenses with an effective focal length of 35mm are also popular as they allow you to get closer to your subjects, but capture more of the scene within the frame. However, to get a focal length of 35mm

on a cropped sensor DSLR you're looking at 24mm prime lenses. To get very wide angles on a cropped DSLR the most cost effective route is likely to be one of the wide-angle zooms, such as Canon's 10–22mm, Nikon's 12–24mm or Sigma's 10–22mm. These are designed specifically for cropped sensor cameras and produce good results. A bonus of a 10–22mm lens is that it is so deceptively wide you can be pointing it away from your subjects, and still capture them within the frame, rendering them oblivious to what you are shooting. The drawback, however, is that these lenses are larger than primes (less discreet) and not as fast.

← Canon 50mm f/1.8 lens
This is a fast, lightweight, and cheap lens, popular with street photographers.

Zoom lenses

The significant advantage of zoom lenses is that thanks to the variation in perspectives and compositions they offer, the photographer has much more flexibility than when shooting with primes.

Historically, zoom lenses were inferior in terms of image quality when compared with primes. But this is no longer so, although high-quality zooms are expensive. Generally speaking good zoom lenses are now on a par with most primes, meaning that you only have to carry a couple of lenses with you to enjoy a focal length range from say 24mm to 300mm, and still achieve exceptional image quality.

↗ **Afternoon Nap—Cork, Ireland**
Canon EOS 20D, 10–22mm ƒ/3.5–4.5 lens
This very wide lens can produce a slightly skewed effect under certain circumstances, like here.

→ **Pigs Are People Too— London, UK**
Canon EOS 20D, 10–22mm ƒ/3.5–4.5 lens
With a lens this wide, it's necessary to get very close to your subjects if you want a tighter crop.

However zoom lenses, particularly long telephoto zooms such as a 70–300mm, are bulky, heavy, and attract a good deal of attention. Furthermore, they go against the street photography ideal of being immersed in and getting up close to the action. Standing so far back from the subject takes away the intimacy that a short focal length prime lens is able to provide.

So which lens?

As you can probably tell by now, street photography is perfectly feasible with all kinds of lenses. We haven't even touched on those that create special effects such as tilt-shift and fisheye lenses, but this section is designed to provide an introduction into commonly used and ideal street photography kit.

What you buy will really depend on what you can afford, and what you are prepared to carry around with you in terms of weight. Although I love the quality of images a 24–70mm ƒ/2.8 lens creates, it is the antithesis of discreet, and it can be tiresome to carry around for hours at a time. In 43°C temperatures and close to 100% humidity in Mumbai, I found that physically I could simply not carry this lens on my DSLR around my neck all day, and found it far more enjoyable to use a smaller film SLR with a prime lens under these conditions.

→ **Street Catwalk—Osaka, Japan**
Canon EOS 350D, 24–70mm ƒ/2.8 lens
A 24–70mm lens is a great all-round versatile lens that allows you to stand far back and zoom into a desired subject or keep it wide, as well as shoot up close, all with an aperture of 2.8. It's just very bulky.

FOUR THIRDS & MICRO FOUR THIRDS

Many photographers want the quality and versatility of a DSLR, without the bulk associated with it. And it was precisely for these photographers that the Four Thirds and Micro Four Thirds systems were developed.

The Four Thirds camera system was first introduced in 2003. Four Thirds cameras work in much the same way as a DSLR, with a reflex mirror and optical viewfinder, but the sensor is around 30–40% smaller than an APS-C sensor. This allows for a smaller camera design and smaller, but still interchangeable, lenses. Although the smaller sensors don't quite match the image quality of standard DSLRs, they are still nine times larger than most point-and-shoot cameras, and are capable of providing clean noise-free images in most daylight conditions.

If you want to go even smaller, following on from the Four Thirds system is the Micro Four Thirds. These cameras utilize the same size sensor as Four Thirds cameras, so are comparable in image quality, but they are mirrorless and therefore don't feature an optical viewfinder, which is why many are similar in size to standard compact point-and-shoot cameras. Image composition is through either an electronic viewfinder or rear LCD screen (or both). Such cameras are ideal for those who want something better than a simple point-and-shoot, but without the weight and bulk of a DSLR.

↑ **Camera—Olympus Pen E-P3 with a 14–42mm lens**
Manufactured: 2011
Type: Micro Four Thirds
Cost: $900
The retro-styling, comprehensive features, and high image quality have made this Olympus Micro Four Thirds camera a popular alternative to larger DSLRs.

Some reasons to consider a Micro Four Thirds camera:

- Small and portable for discreet shooting.
- The digital sensor is larger than those of small compact cameras offering image quality comparable to many DSLRs.
- The ergonomics make these cameras easy to use, hold and function.
- Non-professional appearance doesn't attract attention.

MEDIUM FORMAT

Medium-format cameras take a larger film size (typically 120mm and 220mm) than their 35mm film SLR counterparts. Although these cameras are bulky and often draw looks for their vintage appearance, there are certain medium-format cameras considered to be ideal for street photography, such as the twin lens reflex (TLR) camera, of which a popular model is the Rolleiflex.

This camera differs from an SLR in that it has two lenses of the same focal length; one to take the picture, and one for the viewfinder. The viewfinder is at the top of the camera and is often looked through at waist-level, making picture taking less obvious.

Celebrated street photographer Vivian Maier used a Rollieflex to take tens of thousands of pictures during the 1950s and 1960s, and its success as a street camera is down to a few factors. Despite its size, the Rolleiflex is fairly lightweight, as well as being durable, sturdy, and reliable. The viewfinder is bright and easy to look through, and some Rolleiflex models, such as the Rolleiflex Automat include a mechanical wind mechanism that makes shooting fast-paced action easy.

Although now discontinued, these cameras are sought-after by film and street enthusiasts for their pristine picture quality and reliability. Other TLR brands that are popular in the street world include Mamiya and Yashica. Most TLRs have fixed lenses that could be seen as a disadvantage, but they are generally quiet and unobtrusive. They may receive curious stares for their vintage appearance, but aren't threatening or intimidating.

Most take 120 film, which produces images in a square 6 x 6 format, which is unusual if you are only used to shooting 35mm film.

Aside from TLRs, other reputable medium format cameras include the Mamiya 7 II. This is the only 6 x 7-format rangefinder camera featuring interchangeable lenses. As a rangefinder it has all the qualities necessary for a good street camera—it is lightweight, quiet, and unobtrusive.

→ Camera—Rolleiflex 2.8E with an 80mm *f*/2.8 planar lens
Manufactured: 1956–1959
Type: Medium format film TLR
Cost: $1000, but can vary considerably
Despite their relatively large size, TLR (twin lens reflex) cameras offer outstanding image quality and are popular with a number of professional street photographers.

POINT-AND-SHOOT COMPACT CAMERAS

Point-and-shoot cameras are pocket-sized digital cameras that are slim, lightweight, silent, easily concealable, and straightforward to use. They literally involve pointing and shooting, without having to consider focusing or exposing. This means that as a street photographer, you can put all your energy solely into the subject matter and composition.

Most compact cameras feature an LCD screen for composing, so you can see very clearly what you are capturing, and they are also easy to use from the hip as they are light and small, and only require a click of a button to capture a scene.

← **An Eternal Law—London, UK**
This image was taken on a basic 5 MP compact camera—HP Photosmart R707.

Compact cameras also contain various menus and settings to capture images at night, in bright sunshine, under cloudy conditions, and many others. You simply need to select the appropriate setting, or stick with an auto-setting, and you're good to go.

One crucial aspect for many street photographers is that compact cameras are cheap! But while the image quality of the latest compact digitals has improved, they do have their drawbacks:

Lack of creative control
Compared with an SLR or rangefinder, compacts offer little in terms of DOF and exposure. You'll need to fiddle with settings and menus for anything beyond standard exposure. The scope of these settings is far more limited with compact cameras.

No interchangeable lenses
Although some compacts have a zoom facility, this is often slow, and cumbersome.

Small image sensor
The small image sensors are prone to noise in low-light conditions and only capture wide depth of field.

CAMERA PHONES

Today, it would be unusual not to own a mobile phone. Most of us have one, and while only a few years ago mobile phones were used for making calls, playing the odd game, snapping the occasional low-quality image, and perhaps browsing the internet (with difficulty), today, with the advent of smartphones, a whole new world of possibilities has opened up.

Every mobile phone made today has an in-built camera, and the quality of these is increasing with each new model. In the fast-paced world we live in today, it takes just a couple of clicks to capture a moment, and then to share it with the world. This is highly attractive for those who may not necessarily have access to a computer. It's also a great backup if your other camera stops working for any reason.

Mobile phones have paved the way for instant photography and instant sharing. In many respects they have revolutionized picture taking by encouraging citizen journalism and social media. More than ever before, the once-humble cameraphone has become a powerful tool and is being embraced by all kinds of people, from the young to the old, to the camera-savvy, to the technologically less-inclined.

There are a multitude of applications that can be downloaded to use in conjunction with the camera, and it is no wonder that more people than ever before are using their mobile phones as their primary camera.

What makes a cameraphone so attractive?

- **Small and light**
  You won't get much more compact than this.

- **Accessibility**
  You will almost always have your phone with you, and therefore always have the opportunity to snap a moment.

- **All in one**
  For those who like to carry as little as possible, a mobile phone is a handy device indeed. You can capture an image and within moments edit it if necessary, and share it with the world. You don't need a PC to upload the images to. This is attractive for people who don't have the time or inclination to transfer images. Everything you could want to do with the photo can be done on the phone itself within seconds.

- **Quality**
  While the quality will never be as good as an SLR or rangefinder, the cameraphone today boasts faster speeds and higher resolutions, certainly giving compact cameras a run for their money.

- **Ease of use**
  Cameraphones are point-and-shoot devices—simple to use for those who prefer basic equipment.

↑ **Photographing You—Haridwar, India**
People using their mobile phones to take pictures of me with my DSLR.

← **Playing with Technology— London, UK**
Taken with a Nexus One Google Android phone, using the FXCamera app (free to download) with the ToyCam setting.

→ **Walls—London, UK**
Taken with a Blackberry Bold.

↗ **Canary Wharf—London, UK**
Taken with an iPhone using the popular Hipstamatic app.

→ **Hard Day's Work—London, UK**
The Hipstamatic app imitates the vintage feel of film.

- **Unobtrusive**
  There is no shutter noise associated with a mobile phone camera as sounds can be turned off, allowing you to get as close as you could probably ever get to your subjects without the intimidation factor coming into play. You can also be very discreet as a mobile phone has multiple functions so as far as your subject is concerned you could simply be sending a text, when you are actually taking a photo of them.

- **Apps**
  While cameraphones are basic and don't have interchangeable lenses, there are many apps available that not only edit photos, but also emulate the feel of film, providing a vintage look such as those created with a Polaroid camera.

Smartphone apps

One app that is particularly popular is the Hipstamatic app for the iPhone. This creates "retro" effects that are often characterized by vignetting, high-color contrast, and unusual saturation.

This app allows you to select a film type and lens, snap an image, and also add it to an album and share it with others, including the online Hipstamatic community.

TOY CAMERAS

While smartphone applications can imitate the somewhat retro feel of film, there are a number of cameras on the market that naturally produce these effects and actually use film.

These are very basic, compact, cheap plastic cameras that are appealing for those very qualities. There has been a resurgence of these types of cameras over the past few years. They are popular for their old-school nostalgic look and feel, and they are an authentic alternative to the smartphone applications or editing software that digitally mimics the effects produced by such cameras.

Lomography

Lomography is a term derived from the company LOMO PLC, which produced optics in the Soviet Union. LOMO PLC created a camera called the LOMO LC-A that inspired a company called Lomographische. Lomographische has capitalized on these basic film cameras and has brought them back to life. Their properties make them a popular street photography choice:

- Point-and-shoot
- Usually very cheap
- Lightweight
- Use film

There are a number of 35mm "toy" cameras on the market, such as the plastic TLRs from Blackbird Fly and the Colosplash Lomo camera.

← **Diana-F camera**
The Diana-F camera, and subsequently the Holga, are two medium-format 120-film cameras that are at the core of the Lomography movement.

← **City Snapshot—London, UK**
Taken with Colorsplash Lomo camera
with Fujifilm Superia 400 film.

→ **Man's Best Friend—London, UK**
Taken with Colorsplash Lomo camera
with Fujifilm Superia 400 film.

PINHOLE CAMERAS

Pinhole cameras are the most basic of cameras, and can be home-made very simply with a manually-operated shutter made out of cardboard, making it ideal for the very cash-strapped!

While the results of using such a camera may not yield sharp and clear images, it can nevertheless be used for street photography, and is a fun camera for the more experimental and adventurous. You never really know what kind of photo a pinhole camera is going to produce.

Other types of point-and-shoot film cameras include disposable cameras.

People are unlikely to take these kind of "toy" cameras seriously. They're small, compact, niche, and considered as toys rather than serious photographic equipment. They lack the bells and whistles of any digital camera, rangefinder or SLR, and are certainly not for everyone, but nevertheless they have a surreal quality that makes them desirable for those wishing to put a dream-like spin on everyday life using authentic materials such as film.

← **Camera—Sharan STD 35mm pinhole camera**
This cardboard and plastic camera came with instructions to assemble it to produce a fun and novel device to shoot with.

FILM

The landscape of photography has dramatically changed since the digital camera came into existence. With a wide range of digital equipment available today, film photography is in decline and is arguably a dying medium.

However, one of the genres of photography where film still remains fairly popular is street, and classic cameras such as the rangefinder and film SLRs are keeping the analog photography world alive.

Why film?

Why would anyone want to use film when digital photography is instantly viewable?

Many would argue that using film makes you a better photographer. With a 35mm camera, you have a maximum of 36 frames per roll so unlike with a digital camera you cannot click away mindlessly hoping to capture one good frame from 100. How many times have you snapped the same scene over and over just in case it didn't come out right the first time? Film forces you to think about the image you are about to capture. It makes you far more creative simply because you have to be in order to not waste precious frames. You cannot view the results immediately on an LCD screen as you can with digital photography, which makes you even more careful to produce a fine image the first time round. Therefore over time, you become more competent at composing and shooting, and you

↑ **A selection of 35mm film rolls**
The most commonly used film size is 35mm film. However, other film sizes are available such as 120 and 220 film, designed for medium-format cameras.

are more aware of what works even without having to view the image for validation of this. In short, you just "know" when you've captured a great moment.

Digital photography on the other hand can promote laziness, particularly if shooting with automatic settings. In terms of quality, many argue that the colors and tones produced with film are simply not possible to recreate with digital cameras, and while software such as Photoshop can digitally imitate the tones of film to a degree, this is not quite as satisfying or authentic as producing the same tones within the camera itself with genuine film.

Film developing

Playing the waiting game while your film is being developed is not exactly fun, but there is something exciting about the anticipation of receiving a roll of developed film. In a world of instant gratification, there is something calming about shooting with film. Film fans will also argue that there is something special about holding a developed negative up to the light, compared to simply uploading "flat" digital images to a computer, which could all be lost in a crash.

Which film?

The film you use will depend partly on the camera format. Once you've established the film size, you need to think about when and how you will be shooting.

As 35mm cameras are the most commonly used, it follows that 35mm film is the most accessible; we'll therefore focus on this film type.

As briefly touched upon earlier, film sensitivity varies. You can buy film for very low-light conditions that has a high ISO such as 1600, as well as film for bright sunshine, which will have slower speeds, such as ISO 50, and anything in between. You therefore need to plan ahead and think about where you will be shooting and for how long. To set you in the right direction, ISO 100 and 200 film is good for sunny and bright environments, while ISO 400 is ideal for an overcast winter day. Anything higher is intended for darker scenarios. If your shooting environment and lighting conditions change midway through a roll of film you can technically stop shooting one roll of film, rewind it, take it out, and insert another roll that's more appropriate for the conditions. If necessary you can reinsert the previous roll and advance to where you last finished shooting if the conditions return to their original state. This process has the potential of going horribly wrong if you don't know what you are doing, so be careful if you don't want to lose all the images.

When rewinding a half-exposed roll of film that you'll want to use later, be careful not to rewind the film all the way back into the film canister. Keep a bit of film sticking out of it so that you can use it again. You can often feel less resistance while rewinding as soon as the film pops out of the camera's spool; this is the time to stop rewinding.

When you load the film back into the camera, you'll need to advance it to where you left off. Cover the lens with your hand or put the lens cap on, choose the smallest aperture (i.e. largest f/number) and fastest shutter speed. Then click the shutter button to wherever you left off, e.g. ten images.

COLOR

Another factor to think about is whether you want to shoot in color or black and white. This is down to experimenting and personal preference. Like photography in general, choosing between color and black and white is subjective.

Color

Color is how we see our world, and as such is a natural reflection of our surroundings. Color can be vibrant, captivating, and can add hugely to the general mood and atmosphere of an image.

There are so many hues, tones, and shades around us, that the possibilities of color are almost endless. For me personally I have always embraced the use of color, but this also depends on the weather and where I am. In India, everything to me appears bright, particularly in the sunshine. The streets are visually vivid, bursting with a kaleidoscope of rich tones, and I therefore feel compelled to shoot color film as I feel it's necessary to demonstrate just how powerful and striking the shades in this country are. On the contrary, I tend to use black and white where colors are more subdued or dull, such as on a rainy day in winter in the UK, where I want to bring out the full potential of the different shades of gray around me.

→ **Wash Time—Nashik, India**
Nikon F3, 50mm ƒ/1.8 lens, Kodak Gold 100 film
In bright sunshine, this film always seems to accentuate the richer tones to provide a saturated and bold feel.

Developing color film

Most color film is developed using the C-41 development process. Although not as widespread as it once was, a local photo store should be able to provide a film developing service with a fairly quick turnaround time of a few hours. This differs from black-and-white developing, which many high-street photo stores no longer do. As it's more common, color film is also cheaper to develop in-store than black-and-white film. However, black-and-white film is easier to self-develop at home than color, and is fairly cheap to do so.

Film choice

Color film is widespread and relatively easy to buy in high-street stores. The examples featured in this section are my personal film choices that I use regularly, and I would highly recommend experimenting with various film types to see what works for you. A lot depends on availability. When I travel to India I buy a lot of Kodak film there as it's inexpensive and readily available in local stores compared with cost and availability in the UK. For that reason much of my color film photos are taken with Kodak film.

↗ **Tending the Shop—Nashik, India**
Nikon F3, 50mm *f*/1.8 lens, Kodak Gold 100 film
The colors attracted me to this scene.

→ **Chor Bazzar—Mumbai, India**
Nikon F3, 50mm *f*/1.8 lens, Kodak Ultramax 400 film
This film tends to be a little softer, but still manages to bring out even the dullest shades.

← New Year's—London, UK
Nikon F3, 50mm *f*/1.8 lens, Fujifilm Superia 200 film
Superia 200 works very well outdoors producing sharp images.

↓ Clowns—Ankara, Turkey
Leica M6, 35mm *f*/1.4 lens, Kodak ColorPlus 200 film
ISO 200 film is generally sharper than 400 and ideal for cloudy days and well-lit indoor scenarios.

BLACK & WHITE

Black-and-white (or monochrome) film provides a classic, nostalgic, and often timeless look. It reminds us of the early street photographers who produced some of the most iconic images we know in the world of street photography.

Black and white removes the distraction of color, allowing the subjects to speak for themselves. It reduces visual information to its fundamentals, emphasizing tones, light, and contrast. It's these qualities that make black and white popular with many of today's street photographers. Black-and-white images have more room for interpretation and can often engender more atmosphere and mood within a scene.

← **As The Doors Closed—London, UK**
Nikon EM, 50mm ƒ/1.8 lens, Ilford XP2 Super 400 film
This man spotted me just as the doors on my train were about to close, leaving me with little time to compose. I used a C-41 black-and-white film type, which means that color processing can be used to develop it.

It's a highly versatile medium that adapts well to all situations, from bright sunny days, to wintery nights. Any avid monochrome film shooter will tell you that there is nothing quite like the black-and-white tones of film. It's something you have to experience for yourself to understand.

Developing black-and-white film

Black-and-white film can be processed easily and cheaply at home with the right chemicals and basic equipment. This makes it appealing for those who are money-conscious, but also for those who like to be hands-on. It's quite satisfying playing a part in the entire photographic process, from the picture taking, to the developing itself. In this case you are not just taking photos, but actually making them too.

Photolabs will develop black and white, but these are few and far between today, and you will need to search for local labs that cater for monochrome film. High-street photo stores may have a service for this, but more often than not they will need to send the film off to an external lab so it could take days to get the pictures back. For this reason, the costs to develop the photos from a lab are usually higher than that of color film.

Film choice

Some black-and-white film uses the C-41 development process, which means they can be developed at your local photo store just like color film, and at the same price. Two of these C-41 black-and-white film types are Ilford XP2 Super 400 and Kodak 400CN.

I'm a fan of both of these film types as they produce sharp and clear images without too much grain despite having speeds of 400. They're also ideal for both indoor and slightly dimly-lit places such as the subway, as well as for cloudy outdoor photography.

→ **Man with Falcon in Trafalgar Square—London, UK**
Nikon EM, 24mm ƒ/2.8 lens, Kodak 400CN film
This man's job is to tend to the falcon, which flies around keeping the area clear of pigeons. Black and white is often fabulous for portraits as it strips away all the distractions of color.

← Angel Nigel—London, UK

Nikon FM, 24mm *f*/2 lens, Ilford Delta 400 film

I've come across this man at least five times in London. He generally has a football or tennis racquet with him, and he calls himself Angel Nigel.

↑ Man and Pigeons—London, UK

Nikon FM, 35mm *f*/2.8 lens, Kodak Tri-X 400 film

This film produces a very classic, grainy effect.

← ← The Late Peace Protester Brian Haw—London, UK

Nikon FM, 50mm *f*/1.8 lens, Ilford FP4 125 film

This film produces a very fine grain effect.

← Whirling Dervishes—Istanbul, Turkey

Leica M6, 35mm *f*/1.4 lens, Fujifilm Neopan 1600 film

This film is ideal for low-light situations.

EXPIRED FILM

It may be that you find a selection of films in the attic way past their expiration dates. Instead of chucking these away, you could still use them, but be prepared for some odd and unusual tones and coloring.

To make film last longer and beyond its expiration date, store it in the fridge or freezer, and bring it up to room temperature before use. Although doing this will not completely stop deterioration, it will slow it down considerably.

← **Juhu Beach—Mumbai, India**
Nikon F3, 50mm ƒ/1.8 lens, Kodak Gold 200 film
Juhu Beach can be incredibly crowded, particularly at certain times of the day. I took this shot as there were fewer people around than usual, and the birds were a nice touch. I didn't know what to expect in terms of the color, and as this shows, expired film may not produce the best tones, but they certainly display unique characteristics.

← Subway Ride—London, UK
Nikon F3, 50mm *f*/1.8 lens, Kodak Ultramax 400 film
Expired film here produces unrealistic colors and a
slightly surreal feel to an otherwise very normal scene.

Pushing and pulling film

A film with a particular speed can be "pushed" or up-rated to make it behave like a film with a higher speed. Film can also be "pulled" to behave like film at a slower speed. So, for example, if you have a roll of ISO 400 film, but dark conditions ideally require ISO 800, you can set the ISO to 800 and use it as you would ISO 800 film. When it comes to developing the film, you'll need to develop it for a longer period of time or at a higher temperature. The opposite applies to pull processing. In this instance you'll need to reduce the time the film is developed.

All film manufacturers produce information about how to push/pull process their films, which you can find on the internet. And of course only those who develop their own film will be able to do this.

Useful resources

I'd always recommend buying film at local stores where possible to support the general health of the film photography industry. However, you may sometimes have to check online sources such as eBay.

ACCESSORIES

There's no definitive list of equipment that all street photographers should carry, but sticking to the ethos of street photography, all you should really need with you is a camera and any accessories needed for the camera to function such as batteries, a memory card or film. That's it!

For reasons stated earlier on, a flash is deemed unnecessary as are the likes of tripods or monopods. That's not to say that a tripod or flash should never be used, but for active shooters who have a camera with them at all times, a tripod is an unnecessary commodity taking up space, weight, and energy. A flash could also be highly intimidating for strangers you may be shooting. Always bear this in mind. You don't want to alarm anyone.

If your camera is battery-operated, spare batteries are always useful, as well as ensuring any rechargeable batteries are fully-charged. Cameras with mechanical shutters will continue to function without batteries, but in this case you will need to estimate all the settings such as exposure and shutter speed.

For film shooters, ensure that you have enough rolls of film with you for whatever conditions you are working in, whether for daytime or low light. You don't want to run out of film and waste time looking for it when out shooting. First, you may not find what you want, and secondly, it may well be more expensive to buy in a store than online.

If you are swapping film rolls in mid-use it's handy to keep a CD pen with you to write down the number of frames you have shot on the film canister itself. The last thing you want is to forget how many images you have taken, and then end up shooting over already-exposed frames.

Make sure any camera straps are of the appropriate length and comfortable to use. If you are very tall it may be worth purchasing a separate strap rather than use the one that came with the camera.

With memory cards, ideally you want one with as large a capacity as possible, particularly if you are shooting in Raw mode, which takes up much more space than if you're shooting in standard JPEG format.

If shooting in bad weather, it's always useful to be wearing a hooded top/jacket rather than having to carry an umbrella, which can make shooting difficult if you have to carry that as well as your camera. Depending on your camera, the rain may not affect it allowing you to use it in wet weather. I've used my DSLR in the direct rain of tropical monsoons for short periods of time. If you know you could well be out and about in stormy weather, a plastic carrier bag is useful to have to place over your camera to protect it.

Useful resources
Here are some reputable websites and stores to help you research cameras and other equipment.

General camera information and reviews:
http://www.dpreview.com/
www.cameraquest.com
http://www.fredmiranda.com/

Specialist camera stores and buying second-hand:
www.cameraquest.com (US)
http://www.bhphotovideo.com/ (US)

eBay.com can also be useful for second-hand cameras, but always remember to do research before paying for anything.

↑ **iPhone SLR Mount**
Although somewhat impractical for street photography, it demonstrates that there is much potential for mobile phone cameras. However, at $250, you might just be better off putting the money aside for a new lens or more street-friendly equipment!

5.
DIGITAL PROCESSING

Street photography is a reflection of the world we live in, as you see it through your eyes. Your images are a true representation of the real world, and as such should not need to be heavily post-processed. In this chapter we'll explore some of the most popular techniques used to adjust photos.

CONCEPT OF "GET IT RIGHT"

The aim is to get it right the first time within the camera, not to take the photo and then realize all the settings are incorrect. Street photography should encourage you to compose and expose the scene exactly as you want it, and to embrace the subjects and elements within the frame.

If you don't get it right the first time, learn from your mistakes and keep shooting until you're confident about the settings you're using.

Thinking about this will make you a better photographer. It's thoroughly rewarding to be able to nail an image within the camera itself, and will also mean that you spend less time at your computer making an average image look good, and more time out and about in the field with your camera.

Any post-processing should therefore be simple and straightforward. If you know how to use your camera correctly, these kind of digital enhancements should be kept to a minimum.

Street photography should make you a great photographer with a great eye. You shouldn't need Photoshop to make your photos stand out and create an impact. The photo and subjects should speak for themselves.

→ **Indian Woman—Jaipur, India**
Canon EOS 350D, 24–70mm ƒ/2.8 lens
This image has barely been post-processed. The only editing involved tweaking the levels ever so slightly, but nothing that would dramatically alter the image by any means.

FILE FORMATS

If you're using a digital camera, then there are two common file formats, JPEG (pronounced "jay-peg") and Raw. Both have their advantages and disadvantages.

Advantages of Raw
• Much more flexibility and room for maneuver when it comes to post-processing. So if you capture a scene with all the wrong settings, such as incorrect white balance and 2-stops underexposed, but have shot in the Raw format, there is more of a chance of "saving" it than if you'd shot in JPEG. This is highly advantageous for those shooting in conditions where, for example, the lighting isn't great.

Disadvantages of Raw
• File sizes are much larger than those of JPEG files, so this will invariably take up a lot more space on your memory card. If you plan to be out shooting all day this could be a problem if your card capacity isn't very large.
• Raw files take longer for your camera to process, so if you like continuously shooting in burst mode, for example, this is less feasible.
• JPEG is a universal file type instantly viewable on computers. Raw files need to be processed with specialist software on your computer, which will take some time (although some cameras allow for in-camera Raw conversion).

Dealing with Raw files can therefore be a chore unless you're happy to invest time converting your files and have a fast PC.

Which to use?
In genres of photography such as wedding and concert photography, Raw is logical as you are working under pressure within a time limit and you'll be able to make large adjustments to images that might have been shot incorrectly. You can shoot with less pressure knowing these adjustments can be made later. When someone is relying on you to provide perfect images, shooting in Raw feels a lot safer!

With street, I shoot in JPEG format as it's my personal goal to get my settings correct and I don't like to rely on post-processing heavily. I also prefer spending my time out and about shooting rather than processing Raw files.

To help you decide which format is right for you, if your camera allows it, shoot both in Raw and JPEG at the same time. For the purpose of this chapter I am going to stick with JPEG processing as this is the most common image file type and a universal standard that we all use and recognize.

IMAGE EDITING

Some digital cameras (particularly newer models) feature in-camera editing. This allows you to perform a whole range of editing processes, such as cropping or adjusting colors, while the images are on the camera itself.

This is great when you're on the go and perhaps don't have access to a computer. The disadvantage of this is that you'll be editing on a small LCD screen, which may not make for particularly accurate edits. An image can look perfectly in focus on your camera's LCD screen, but as soon as you view it on a computer screen, the imperfections really show up.

Editing software

The most prolific image-editing software is Adobe Photoshop—a powerful editing tool used by professionals the world over. However, the program is extremely expensive, and far too complex for most users, particularly if you're only intending to undertake minor adjustments.

A cut-down and much more affordable option is Photoshop Elements. This software is powerful enough to perform the most complex image-editing tasks, but like Photoshop you'll need to devote a lot of time learning how to get the most from it.

Adobe Lightroom is another less expensive option, and is designed specifically with photographers in mind, and in that respect it is more intuitive than either Photoshop or Elements, with a shorter learning curve. Additionally, as well as being able to perform all but the most localized, pixel-based editing, Lightroom is also an efficient image organizer. You can easily arrange your images into folders, add key words, tags, and other metadata, making it easy to set up and maintain an image library.

Other excellent image-editors include Corel Paint Shop Photo Pro, Serif Photo Plus, Ulead Photoimpact, and many more. You can download free trial versions of most programs and try them for yourself.

Free software

There is an increasing number of editing programs available for free. Gimp, which is similar in appearance to Photoshop, is perhaps the best known, and is available at www.gimp.org. Pixlr (www.pixlr.com) is a great editing website that allows you to upload an image and adjust it via the website's interface itself, so you don't actually have to download anything. It's fast, intuitive, and ideal if you are using another PC that doesn't have any photo-editing software on it. It also provides a free Android and iPhone smartphone application called Pixlr-o-matic.

Other free software includes Photoscape and Paint.NET to name just two. Again, a quick search on the internet will throw up all sorts of alternatives. Over the next few pages we'll be looking at some basic image-editing tasks.

CROPPING

There are debates within street photography as to the extent that you should crop your images. While some believe that an image should include everything that was intended within the frame, there will be times when you regret the original composition and framing. Similarly, if you had to grab the shot in a hurry or from the hip, you may also end up reviewing the image and realize that it would look far better cropped in some way.

↓ London Marathon—London, UK
Canon EOS 350D, 18–55mm ƒ/3.5–5.6 lens
This is the original photo I captured at the London Marathon. When I downloaded the image to my computer, I realized I wasn't keen on the empty space to the left of the image, and the white banner on the bottom left was far too distracting for my liking.

↑ Step 1
Using the Crop tool, I selected the area of the image that I wanted to keep.

↓ Step 2
To retain the 35mm dimensions of the image, I further cropped it from the bottom.

← Step 3
The resulting image involves a tighter crop, removing the empty space and most of the distracting banner.

↙ Step 4
We can go even further to remove the white banner completely, make the crop even tighter. This crop incorporates the rule of thirds, placing the main subject in the bottom left-hand third of the image.

→ Step 5
When it comes to cropping, you can totally transform an image. In this instance I have decided I want a vertical frame rather than a horizontal one.

Which do you prefer?
Cropping provides the option of being able to eliminate distracting and unsightly features, as well as opening up the possibility of framing options that you may not have been able to consider at the time. Street photography can be very fast moving, so while ideally you want to capture the frame perfectly, cropping allows you to digitally cut off unnecessary or unwanted aspects of an image for greater impact.

ROTATING

Sometimes you may find that the alignment of horizontal and vertical elements is ever so slightly off, which clearly wasn't an intentional look you were going for. You can easily straighten these up with editing software.

↓ **Step 1**

To straighten the image, start by going to Select > All. Next go to Edit > Transform > Rotate. Now, when you move the cursor to one of the corners of the image it will become a double-ended arrow. Use this to rotate the image until it's straight.

When the image is straight, you'll need to use the Crop tool to remove the white areas that will have appeared on the screen as you've rotated the image.

↑ **If Only—Jerusalem, Israel**
Canon EOS 350D, 18–55mm ƒ/1.8 lens
In this example, the image is not straight, which isn't ideal in terms of composition and framing.

 Before

 After

As this example proves, rotating even very slightly can have a huge impact on an image. When you are shooting, it's important to try and get the horizon straight, particularly where buildings are concerned.

CURVES

The Curves command is one of the most powerful tools available in Photoshop and other image-editors. It is used to adjust tone and contrast, two elements central to the aesthetic qualities of an image.

→ Original image
This image is flat, with subdued colors, and lacks tonal range and contrast.

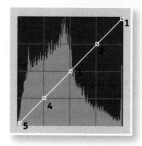

← The Curves dialog
At the heart of the Curves control is a diagonal line that represents the various tones present in the image, as shown here. By clicking and dragging the line either up or down it's possible to alter the tones in those specific areas.

1. White Point
2. Highlights
3. Midtones
4. Shadows
5. Black Point

↓ Step 1
Moving the midtones upwards brightens the entire image.

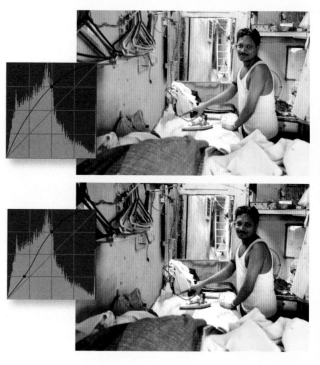

↑ Step 2
Having brightened the midtones, we can now click on a point in the shadow region and drag it downwards. This adds contrast to the image.

As well as adjusting tones and contrast, Curves can also be used to fix incorrect white balance.

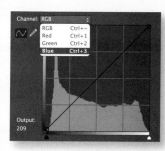

→ **Original image**
In this image, there is a distinctly unflattering blue hue as a result of incorrect white balance. I was also using expired film and everything else on the roll also had a slightly "off" look. This was the most extreme of the frames on the roll.

← **Step 1**
To correct this, bring up the Curves dialog again, but this time select Blue from the Channel drop-down box.

↙ **Step 2**
I also selected the Green, Red, and default RGB options, and tweaked the diagonal lines up and down until I was happy with the resulting image.

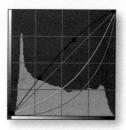

→ **Final image**
With these quick adjustments the image now looks far more natural.

DODGING & BURNING

The Dodge and Burn tools allow you to respectively lighten and darken parts of your image. They can be used effectively to improve contrast, color, and to emphasize certain elements within the picture. Once a traditional darkroom technique, dodging and burning is still valid in today's digital environment.

Burning

Select the Burn tool from the Tool panel. In the Tool options bar at the top of the workspace, you have the option of selecting the brush size and opacity, and also whether you want to burn on highlights, midtones or shadows. I generally burn on the midtones and highlights for more contrast, but the settings you use will depend on the image and what you are trying to achieve. Experiment with these options to see how they impact your image.

↑ Original image
The original image didn't pack sufficient punch. Burning is a good tool to use if the image appears washed out.

↑ Adjusted image
I used the Burn tool set to Highlights and Midtones to selectively darken certain areas. The outcome shows more texture on the walls behind the subject. The colors where the burning has been applied are also darker making them bolder and more accentuated.

Dodging

Dodging is the opposite of burning, in that parts of the image are being made lighter; but like burning, dodging can be used to accentuate elements of an image.

→ **Carnival Girl— London, UK**
Canon EOS 350D, 50mm *f*/1.8 lens
This spontaneous portrait was taken during a Latino carnival where this girl was performing. However, her eyes didn't sparkle as much as I wanted them to.

→ → **Adjusted image**
So I used the Dodge tool to brighten the eyes, which lifts the portrait greatly.

ANTONIO NAVARRO WIJKMARK

BRIAN QUENTIN WEBB

CHARLOTTE GONZALEZ

CLAIRE ATKINSON

DANNY SANTOS II

FELIX LUPA

FERHAT ÇELIK

MUSTAFAH ABDULAZIZ

RONYA GALKA

SEAMUS TRAVERS

SEVERIN KOLLER

6.
SHOWCASE

Street photography can be shot on any camera, anywhere. From the humble mobile phone, to the traditional rangefinder camera, the photographers featured in this showcase represent a pool of talent and illustrate a variety of styles of this raw and real form of photography.

Each of these skilled and passionate photographers provide valuable insight into their thought processes when shooting street, elaborating on tactics, equipment choices, and approaches to shooting. Some shoot exclusively in cities, others immerse themselves in the suburban world. Some shoot solely in black and white with perfected tones, while others embrace the vibrancy of color. I hope you enjoy their work.

ANTONIO NAVARRO WIJKMARK

LOCATION: **BARCELONA, SPAIN**
WEBSITE: **WWW.WIJKMARKPHOTO.COM**

I was born in Barcelona and studied architecture, subsequently studying architectural projects in several studios. My photography was beginning to take up more and more of my time so I decided to dedicate myself to it and turned professional in 2008. I've worked on numerous assignments relating to architectural photography, portraits, advertising campaigns, and industrial photography, but the thing that really keeps me going is street photography.

How did you get into street photography?
Street is the best studio to improve photographic techniques, so I think I got into it when someone gave me my first Canon film camera, and I started shooting slide film, looking for anonymous models on the streets of Barcelona.

What would you say is your style? What makes you stand out?
I'm not trying to create any particular style at all, because I feel that if you acquire a set style, people will expect and ask that of you, and I prefer not to be tied to any niche of street photography. Great photographers change their styles and adapt and are flexible, and that is what I am striving and aiming to be. I'm not a purist in street photography either. I don't like to simply document reality, but rather to somehow distort it by trying to capture weird and wonderful situations, and to reinvent people's lives and their stories beyond reality.

What equipment do you use?
I left the film world in 2004, tired of the amount of money I was spending striving for perfection in my images. When I bought my first digital camera, everything changed. I recognize the advantage of film and its tones and quality, and I intend to return to this, but I'm happily shooting with a DSLR—a Canon EOS 40D. It's certainly heavy, noisy, and at times uncomfortable, but it's affordable and produces great results. In terms of lenses I own the following Canon lenses: 10–22mm f/3.5–4.5, 85mm f/1.8, and a 50mm f/1.4. I occasionally rent other lenses too.

↑ Next Round—Barcelona, Spain
Canon EOS 40D, 10–22mm ƒ/4 lens, 1/8 second, ISO 500

↓ I'm Lovin' It—Barcelona, Spain
Canon EOS 40D, 10–22mm ƒ/4 lens, 1/8 second, ISO 500

← Gravity's Law—Barcelona, Spain
Canon EOS 40D, 85mm ƒ/1.8 lens, 1/6400 second, ISO 250

↓ Vacancy—Barcelona, Spain
Canon EOS 40D, 10–22mm ƒ/4.5 lens, 1/32 second, ISO 800

↑ Random Threesome—Barcelona, Spain
Canon EOS 5D Mark II, 70–200mm ƒ/3.5 lens, 1/80 second, ISO 400

↑ Define Paradise II—Barcelona, Spain
Canon EOS 40D, 10–22mm ƒ/3.5 lens, 1/2500 second, ISO 100

↓ When the City Smiles—Barcelona, Spain
Canon EOS 40D, 10–22mm ƒ/4 lens, 1/2500 second, ISO 100

How I made *Lucifer 2.0*

I went hunting one Friday afternoon with my DSLR and a new rented lens that I wanted to try—a Canon 24mm *f*/1.4. I live near the center of Barcelona, so I started in Plaza Catalunya, where many human stories take place.

I was looking around with all my senses connected, but without seeing anything interesting to be captured. Suddenly, I saw someone that caught my attention—a man inside a stationary escalator. I approached him without knowing exactly why he was there, just lifting up my camera to be ready to shoot. I chose a vertical frame to emphasize the size and shape of the escalator, knowing that these kind of moments can disappear in seconds. He seemed to be repairing the escalator with a screwdriver in his hand. I shot once, and he turned his face to me with a mix of surprise and anger. While I was still looking through the viewfinder, it seemed he was thinking, "Have you never seen a man inside an escalator before?" (I must confess no!) I then reacted like I have done all the other times I've been caught by the subject. I slowly slid the camera down to let him look at my eyes and the direction my gaze was pointed to, which was now fixed on the four girls chatting above him. The rules of street photography psychology and experience tell me that when you do that, the subject will then look at what he assumes you were photographing. So he lifted up his head and looked at the four girls, and I shot again. That was when lady luck appeared on the scene. She walked a few steps down as if she was looking for a late date inside the station. I looked at him, he looked at me again, and I then looked at her, knowing he would follow my gaze to her. I then lifted up the camera and quickly clicked! There is the virtual diagonal line in the composition that balances the three subjects in the scene, there is the desire in his eyes, and the wonder in hers. Now the title, *Lucifer 2.0*, and the story comes together.

A great way I chose to learn street photography is by looking at the masters' film strips and trying to envisage why they choose their particular frame from ten or 20 of the same scene. People still think that a good street photograph is a lucky thousandth of a second in time, but luck is just a part of a big pie made of patience, prediction, human psychology, passion, and finally, a little bit of art.

→ **Lucifer 2.0—Barcelona, Spain**
Canon EOS 40D, 24mm ƒ/1.4 lens, 1/1000 second, ISO 400

SHOWCASE
BRIAN QUENTIN WEBB

LOCATION: **TAIPEI, TAIWAN**
WEBSITE: **WWW.PHOTOJAZZ.WS**

I'm an American expat who has been working primarily as an educator in Taipei, Taiwan for about a dozen years now. I originally moved to Taipei as a software engineer and when that contract ended, I decided to stay. I have been photographing people doing people things since I was 12 years old.

How did you get into street photography?
I got into street photography as an evolution from one of my favorite childhood activities—going with my mom or dad to Venice Beach, California for an afternoon of "People Watching." I took a temporary break from it when I started my "professional life," but returned to regular street photography on moving from Los Angeles to Taipei as a way to absorb, explore, and translate the rather large cultural shift—and I haven't stopped since.

What would you say is your style? What makes you stand out?
I actively look for juxtapositions and opposites as I'm making photos. I also love front-to-back compositions with different elements that give an image some depth, even without the benefit of a wide-angle lens. I think those two elements combined make up a coherent "style." I also love rainy days and so many of my images reflect this.

What equipment do you use?
My primary camera for the past couple of years has been the Olympus E-P2. It's something that fits easily in my bag and it's small enough not to draw attention. With it I normally use the Olympus 17mm $f/2.8$, but like many photographers, I'm lusting after the faster Panasonic 20mm $f/1.7$ lens. I also like to use my mobile phone a lot, and in particular the HTC Desire HD. I treat phone photography as the digital equivalent of the Holga/LOMO and choose and compose my subjects as if it were. I also have a Cosina-Voigtlander Bessa R2a with a 35mm lens.

← Typhoon Krosa—Taipei, Taiwan
Cosina-Voigtlander Bessa R2a, 35mm *f*/1.4 lens,
unrecorded exposure, Kodak Tri-X 400 film

**→ Hsimen
Market—
Taipei, Taiwan**
Olympus E-P2,
17mm *f*/4 lens,
1/200 second, ISO
200 (post-
processed with
Nik's Snapseed)

**↑ Afternoon Rain From the
Back of a Taxi—Taipei, Taiwan**
Olympus EP-2, 17mm *f*/4 lens, 1/125 second,
ISO 200

**↑ Taiwanese Pet-owner—
Taipei, Taiwan**
Vignette for Android, "toy camera"
settings

↑ Toys 'R Us—Taipei, Taiwan
RetroCam+ for Android, "FudgeCan"
settings

**↑ Chinese Lantern—Sanxia Old
Street, Taiwan**
Olympus E-P2, 17mm *f*/4 lens, 1/400
second, ISO 200 (post-processed using
Nik's Snapseed for iPad)

↑ Spring Rain—Taipei, Taiwan
Olympus E-P2, 17mm *f*/4.5 lens, 1/125
second, ISO 200 (post-processed using
Nik's Snapseed for iPad)

How I made *Safe Haven*

There are always a couple of typhoons that hit Taiwan every year. Jangmi in 2008 happened to be a big one and forced all shops and services to cease for a day—all shops and services except for 7-11 and Starbucks, that is. About halfway through the afternoon, out of sheer boredom, my wife decided that she wanted cake and coffee, and decided that it would be nice for me to brave the Force-4 typhoon in order to get it for her.

Me being a lover of all days rainy jumped at the excuse to risk my life in exchange for the opportunity to get some great photos and a latte. I made it the three blocks to the neighborhood Starbucks, manned by one *barista* behind the counter and two with brooms at the front door to sweep out the water as the door opened when people entered and exited. What struck me was the stark difference between the chaos going on outside and the relative ease and calmness of the patrons sipping their drinks inside. A group of very elderly women sitting in one corner made me question Newtonian physics as I tried to comprehend how they'd got from their homes to the café!

I wanted to try and capture that juxtaposition in one frame because it was such a poignant one. Just photographing the customers wouldn't accomplish that goal as it wouldn't include the mess outside. The obvious answer to that was the large glass window that separated the typhoon outside with the coffee-drinking inside. Thankfully, there was a customer already sitting there. The only other thing I needed was a clear visual sign to convey the power of the weather outside. Like Howard Hughes waiting for clouds before filming air combat scenes in *Hell's Angels* to better illustrate the speed of the aircraft, I needed a cue. Being located on an intersection, the glass window faced a crosswalk, so I only needed to be patient and wait for someone to cross, then be sure to time it correctly.

→ **Safe Haven—Typhoon Jangmi, Taipei, Taiwan**
Cosina-Voigtlander Bessa R2a, 35mm *f*/1.4 lens, unrecorded exposure, Kodak Tri-X 400 film

CHARLOTTE GONZALEZ

LOCATION: **PARIS, FRANCE**
WEBSITE: **HTTP://GONZALE.NET**

Born in 1985, I graduated from high school in Literature and Arts. After attending a five-year program in the Parisian Fine Arts school l'Ecole Nationale Supérieure des Arts Décoratifs, I graduated in 2010 with the highest mention (Félicitations du Jury) for my work on Beirut, *Breaches*. I focus on daily life and youth, traveling between the Middle East and Europe, and am currently based in Paris.

How did you get into street photography?
I think I was around 14 when I took my first street photograph. There was a photography class in my junior high school in Beirut and the first assignment was to go in the street and take pictures of people and places. I remember taking my mother's film camera and shooting portraits of strangers, lights and shadows on walls, plastic bags in trees and modern ruins. When I think of this, I realize my approach hasn't changed a lot, but my technique has got better and I know more precisely what I want to build throughout my images. At the time I was just expressing my sense of observation, and I would say that it is the first attribute to have when shooting street: a good sense of observation.

What would you say is your style? What makes you stand out?
What I have learned over the years is to show things simply with very few elements and yet make the spectator feel something beyond what can be seen—not always a metaphor. My street photographs are more about the empathy one may feel toward my subject, rather than kindly mocking them. I'm also looking for patterns, lights, contrasts, moods, strange or ordinary as long as they speak to me.

What equipment do you use?
For a couple of years now I've been shooting with a Canon EOS 5D (Mark I). It's not a very discreet camera, but with a small lens, such as the Canon 35mm $f/2$ or the 50mm $f/1.8$, it's not too imposing and somehow people don't notice me, even when I'm very close. I occasionally use a Leica M6 rangefinder, with which I also use a 35mm lens.

← Woman Lost in her Thoughts—Parisian Metro, France
Canon EOS 5D, 35mm *f*/2 lens, 1/1600 second, ISO 50

← People Celebrating the Enlargement of a Bar—Beirut, Lebanon
Canon EOS 5D, 35mm *f*/2 lens, 1/60 second, ISO 1250

↑ Girl Smoking in Front of a Gallery—Paris, France
Canon EOS 5D, 50mm *f*/1.8 lens, 1/2500 second, ISO 400

→ Woman Running to Catch a Suburban Train—Paris, France
Canon EOS 5D, 35mm *f*/2 lens, 1/500 second, ISO 640

← Girl Checking her Phone in the Smoking Room of a Club—Paris, France
Canon EOS 5D, 35mm *f*/2 lens, 1/180 second, ISO 1250

→ Girl in an Advertising Vehicle and her Two Colleagues Walking Away—Beirut, Lebanon
Canon EOS 5D, 35mm *f*/2 lens, 1/80 second, ISO 640

← Girl Smoking Outside of her University in New York City—NY, USA
Pentax ME Super, 50mm *f*/2.8 lens, Fuji Reala 100

How I made *Pigeons*

The way I shoot street is always different from one shot to another. Sometimes I choose a frame and wait for things to happen in it, sometimes I see something afar and run after it to get a shot, and sometimes I even go to a place knowing exactly what image I want to take. But most of the time, I just stumble upon things, and if I'm quick enough, I get a good photograph. This is the case with this frame.

This view is the same one I've had almost every day when taking the suburban train to Paris, and usually it's the most boring thing to glance at. But I always carry a camera with me, and on that cold day of January 2009 I took it out of my bag as soon as I saw the pigeons, crossed a fence, and quickly positioned myself to have a properly balanced frame. I waited a second for the birds to move to the center of the beam, then everything was aligned and I pressed the shutter release. Now of course, luck was on my side and I can't say I was certain to capture the birds in this pose, but I like to rely on luck at least a little bit; I could have missed this shot, but I didn't and it ended up on my memory card. Doing street photography is a little bit like a Zen activity. Your head has to be empty, and you have to be ready to receive whatever comes to you. Whenever I think too much about what I should take photos of, or on the contrary when I'm too distracted, I'm not productive. I have to be aware of what surrounds me (listening is sometimes key) without actively "looking" for things. And when I do see something that I feel will be interesting, I have to know my equipment perfectly to be able to get the best possible shot—and let luck do its thing. It's all about being in control and not in control at the same time.

Moments before I took this photograph, I wasn't expecting anything. And as soon as I saw what was happening, I knew what frame I wanted out of it. Or more precisely I envisaged something would happen and gave myself the opportunity. I built the frame and let luck fill the content. Now, of course, it is just a photograph of two pigeons. But photography turned them into a butterfly.

→ **Pigeons—Paris, France**
Canon EOS 5D, 50mm ƒ/1.8 lens, 1/2000 second, ISO 150

SHOWCASE
CLAIRE ATKINSON

LOCATION: **MANCHESTER, UK**
WEBSITE: **WWW.CLAIREATKINSON.NET**

I got into photography at 16. I had dropped out of higher education and was working in a supermarket. Suddenly losing 40 hours a week made me appreciate my spare time, so on my days off I would go on trips and take photographs as souvenirs. As I grew more curious about photography, I discovered the work of Robert Frank. I have never looked back since.

What would you say is your style?
Many argue that great street photographs depict scenes that dissolve immediately after the exposure. However, it is worth remembering that life frozen at 1/250th of a second may not be a true representation of reality.

I endeavor to make pictures that are about more than just irony. I seek the things that sit there all day, unnoticed, waiting to be swept away with the tide of city life in all its chaos and monotony.

What equipment do you use?
I use an old Leica M6 rangefinder with 35/40mm lenses. I am not a fan of digital—I personally find it disposable and predictable. I love the surprise of using film.

→ Ladies on Dale Street—Manchester, UK
Leica M6, 35mm ƒ/2 lens, Kodak Gold 200

↓ Wheelchair—Manchester, UK
Konica Hexar AF, 35mm ƒ/2 lens, Kodak Tri-X 400

↓ Dog on Oxford Street—London, UK
Cosina-Voigtlander Bessa R2a, 50mm ƒ/2 lens, Kodak Tri-X 400

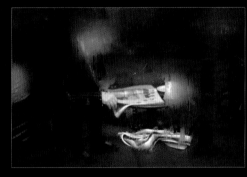

↑ Steamy Window 2—Manchester, UK
Leica M6, 50mm ƒ/2 lens, Kodak Portra 160

↑ Mummy by the Seine—Paris France
Konica Hexar AF, 35mm ƒ/2 lens, Fuji Sensia 200

← Hand in Shadow—Istanbul, Turkey
Leica M6, 40mm ƒ/2 lens, Kodak Portra 160

↑ Arse—Istanbul, Turkey
Leica M6, 40mm ƒ/2 lens, Kodak Portra 160

How I made *Steamy Window 1*

I captured this scene in December 2010. I had just finished an early morning shift at work and I headed into the center of Manchester to meet a friend to explore the Christmas markets together. After walking around aimlessly for a while and experiencing the same overpriced, over crowded stuff as last year, we began to head away from the square.

From the other side of the road, I noticed the windows of the nearest Starbucks had completely steamed up. It was freezing outside. I'm no fan of chain-store ambience, but I couldn't help noticing how cosy it looked from where I was standing. I told my friend I had to go over and check it out.

I circled the two sides of the shop and went around the front and peered in the windows. I knew there was a photograph within this scene, but I couldn't figure out where. I noticed a small area of condensation had been rubbed from the inside, providing me with a little peep hole of my own. I got closer and shifted around until my eyes were level with the gap. I saw something pink inside—a huge baby! I moved until she filled the little gap perfectly and I raised my camera. I didn't have time to think properly, but I pre-visualized the

final image as I always do. I stood back slightly to bring in more of the window and steam, and to further isolate the kid, and shot three frames.

It can be difficult focusing on a small area like this on a rangefinder, so I wasn't giving myself room for any mistakes.

When I scanned the negatives, I was happy to see the picture had come out just as I had pre-visualized. Someone even remarked that it looks like the baby is floating, which I love.

→ **Steamy Window 1—Manchester, UK**
Leica M6, 50mm ƒ/2 lens, Kodak Portra 160

When I picked up my first camera in mid-2008, I didn't know what I wanted to shoot. I just knew I wanted to shoot. So I shot just about everything, from cats, flowers, landscapes, to sunsets. That was until I discovered street photography on Flickr. I knew right there and then that's what I wanted to do. The feeling of photographs being so raw and real just appealed to me so much. So I researched and discovered the masters in street photography like Garry Winogrand, William Klein, Daido Moriyama, Trent Parke, and Philip-Lorca diCorcia. I've been hooked since then. Though I didn't really follow their styles, it served as a great jump-off point showing me the possibilities that street could provide.

What would you say is your style? What makes you stand out?

I guess the one thing that makes me stand out is my preference for the 85mm focal length. I know using a wide-angle lens is more preferred when it comes to traditional street photography, but I sort of like the voyeuristic aesthetic that a slightly longer lens provides.

I still do occasionally use a wide-angle lens (20mm), in fact, I find it easier to use since you're not constrained with space and you capture a whole lot more. I just don't want to restrict myself with using a particular focal length when shooting in the street, and I like to be able to mix it up. I also like to experiment shooting in bad weather. Rain to me presents a unique atmosphere and has the potential to bring out interesting human drama.

One of the projects that gained quite a bit of publicity for me was my "Portraits of Strangers" set where I took close-up portraits of people who I found stood out of the crowd. Although this isn't considered street photography *per se* since these were taken with permission, for me it still epitomizes the spirit of street photography because it tries to capture the subject's character and essence without pretensions or any form of preparation while still retaining the subject's anonymity and mystery.

What equipment do you use?

A Nikon D300, an 85mm *f*/1.4 lens, and a 20mm *f*/2.8 lens.

↓ Silhouette of Woman Walking in Light—Orchard Road, Singapore
Nikon D300, 20mm ƒ/2.8 lens, 1/125 second, ISO 560

← Cleaner Juxtaposed with Big Christian Dior Billboard—Orchard Road, Singapore
Nikon D300, 85mm ƒ/1.4 lens, 1/8000 second, ISO 200

↓ Girl in Blue Dress—Orchard Road, Singapore
Nikon D300, 85mm ƒ/1.4 lens, 1/6400 second, ISO 200

↑ Stranger #7, from "Portraits of Strangers" project—Orchard Road, Singapore
Nikon D300, 85mm ƒ/1.4 lens, 1/125 second, ISO 450

↑ Two Girls Running Barefoot in the Rain—Orchard Road, Singapore
Nikon D300, 85mm ƒ/1.4 lens, 1/250 second, ISO 200

↘ Man on Bike with Smiling Umbrella—Orchard Road, Singapore
Nikon D300, 85mm ƒ/1.4 lens, 1/400 second, ISO 200

↑ Man in Singlet Walking in the Crowd—Orchard Road, Singapore
Nikon D300, 85mm ƒ/1.4 lens, 1/3200 second, ISO 200

How I made *Silhouette in the Rain*

I love photographing strangers in bad weather. I think the rain provides an opportunity for atmospheric and dramatic scenes. In this photo, it was one of the heaviest rains I've ever shot in. Even with my umbrella, I was completely soaked, to the point where I was even worried that I might have wrecked my iPhone as it was totally drenched inside my pocket. But seeing the picturesque atmosphere brought out by the street lights under the rain, I knew I had a potential keeper just waiting to happen. So I moved on.

While I was standing in the intersection, crossing paths with pedestrians hurrying to get to shelter, I noticed this lone figure from afar… right in the middle of Orchard Road. The silhouette was walking away from where I was, so with my tiny umbrella in one hand and camera in the other, I ran toward it to catch a better look. Suddenly I realized the figure was actually walking in my direction! I hurriedly backed up until I got the framing I wanted. I knelt down, pointed, and just clicked away.

When the figure walked past me, I realized it was an old lady. She was just casually walking, braving the heaviest of rains, with the whole street to herself. What a big contradiction to the younger crowd I usually encounter, hurrying to get to shelter like the rain was a bad thing.

→ **Silhouette in the Night Rain—Orchard Road, Singapore**
Nikon D300, 85mm ƒ/1.4 lens, 1/125 second, ISO 200

SHOWCASE
FELIX LUPA

LOCATION: **TEL AVIV, ISRAEL**
WEBSITE: **WWW.FELIXLUPA.COM**

I am a second generation photographer born in the Ukraine, in the former Soviet Union. I've been a freelance photographer since 1995, working with Israel's leading newspapers. I've worked on numerous long-term social projects for magazines and television, and have been exhibited in various local and international exhibitions.

Recently I decided to dedicate myself to street photography to serve as the "public eye," conveying messages from the streets. The ability to see and connect with human situations is like a basic instinct—almost like breathing. The public eye is the medium through which I am able to express my point of view.

How did you get into street photography?
It's seven years since I realized the photographs I was posting on the internet were street photographs. No doubt I would have missed this wonderful genre, had it not been for my late exposure to the internet. So I decided to adopt it whole-heartedly. Picture by picture it has revealed to me how amazing the street is; full of thrilling human experiences.

I still hurry to the street like a little boy to his playground. It is my imagination that insists on a personal style, the fingerprint unique to each photographer. A lot of time, patience, and a great deal of contact with different people are necessary until one acquires the ability to maneuver successfully in the street. Unique ways of seeing, the ability to analyze a situation, and react quickly to it, are the tools the street photographer carries with him.

What equipment do you use?
I use a Sony DSC S600, a Leica D-LUX 3, and a Ricoh GX100.

→ The Mannequin—Israel
Ricoh Caplio GX100, 6mm *f*/3.7 lens,
1/620 second, ISO 100

**↓ Stance—
Israel**
Sony DSC-S600,
5mm *f*/2.8 lens,
1/100 second,
ISO 80

**↑ The Beach—
srael**
Sony DSC-S600,
5mm *f*/6.3 lens,
/1000 second,
SO 80

**→ For a
Walk—Israel**
Sony DSC-S600,
5mm *f*/6.3 lens,
/160 second,
SO 80

↑ Air Walk—Israel
Sony DSC-P100, 15mm *f*/8 lens, 1/200 second, ISO 100

**↑↑ Lick—
Israel**
Sony DSC-S600,
5mm *f*/6.3 lens,
1/640 second,
ISO 80

**↑ This Way—
Israel**
Sony DSC-S600,
5mm *f*/6.3 lens,
1/640 second,
ISO 80

How I made *A Run*

An elderly man with a walking stick at the beach seemed a bit unusual that day and I decided to follow him to see what developed next.

This lasted an hour along the beach when suddenly in the distance I saw a young man running toward me. I immediately understood that this was the picture I had to capture—that it would symbolize contrast and contradiction between young and old.

I had about 10 seconds to design the frame. I timed the pace of the older man's walk compared with the young running man, and I calculated the meeting point between them in my mind.

I realized that if the man running saw the camera he would try to run outside of my frame. Immediately I overtook the older man by several feet and leaned on the sand to "tie my shoelace." I used this tactic to deflect attention from me and my camera; when I got down I continued to estimate the young man's strides toward me. At the crucial moment the older man passed me and came right to that meeting point between the two of them as I predicted. One shot from low down was enough for me to capture the moment I had envisaged and waited for.

→ **A Run—Israel**
Sony DSC-S600, 5mm ƒ/2.3 lens, 1/640 second, ISO 80

SHOWCASE
SHOWCASE
FERHAT ÇELIK

LOCATION: **LONDON, UK**
WEBSITE: **WWW.FERHATCELIK.CO.UK**

I was born in Turkey in 1972 and have been living in London since 1995. My appetite for learning helped me to master my skills as a photographer as I am completely self-taught. My skills as an observer give me the edge on creativity. City life, road signs, and landmarks are all part of my chosen backgrounds and play major roles in my compositions. I have a unique tonal range and I enjoy using human elements in my photos with geometric details from the environment. I wander the streets for hours on end to find the right location and the elements required to make my photos. My aim is to introduce the viewer to the locations that I am photographing, and wherever this may be, I strive to bring to others unusual compositions and perspectives.

How did you get into street photography?
My love for street photography began in 2004 when I got my camera (a Canon 20D with an 18–55mm lens). At first I wasn't sure what to do with it, but with practice, I gained confidence and it felt kind of liberating—being free on the streets capturing moments all around me.

What would you say is your style? What makes you stand out?
The use of human elements in my photographs with geometric details from the environment gives me my signature look, as well as the tones I consistently use in my photos.

What equipment do you use?
I use a Canon 5D MkII with 16–35mm f/2.8, 50mm f/1.4, 24–105mm f/4, and 70–20mm f/4 lenses; and a Leica M6 with 21mm f/2.8 and 24mm f/2.8 lenses.

← 4739—London, UK
Canon 40D, 17–85mm
f/6.3 lens, 1/100 second,
ISO 200

← ← 4175—
London, UK
Leica M6, 24mm
f/2.8 lens

↑ 4444—London, UK
Canon 40D, 17–85mm f/14 lens,
1/50 second, ISO 200

← 4200—London, UK
Canon 40D, 17–85mm
f/3.5, 1/125 second,
ISO 250

↑ 159—London, UK
Canon 30D, 17–85mm
f/8 lens, 1/125 second,
ISO 200

← 4468—London, UK
Canon 40D, 17–85mm f/4.5 lens,
1/320 second, ISO 200

↑ 4003—Istanbul, Turkey
Leica M6, 21mm f2.8 lens, Ilford
Delta 100 film

How I made *Headrush*

I took this photo on the banks of the River Thames in London. Whenever I went out to take photographs I used to have a quick look at this area. I was fascinated by the geometric details and the human traffic consisting of people going about their daily lives, almost like robots. Although I have captured images in the same place before, I hadn't previously noticed this movement of people.

After a couple of unsatisfactory shots I decided to wait. 45 minutes had passed when I captured this shot, and for me it was most definitely worth the long wait.

With all my photographs, I first choose the background and then wait for the character I imagine in my mind to come into the frame. Even if I do not initially envisage what the shot will look like, my stubbornness gets the better of me and I get a result even if it means going back another day. As a street photographer, I believe patience and observation are key strengths, and these are two qualities that any good street photographer should acquire.

→ **Headrush—London, UK**
Canon 30D, 17–85mm *f*/5.6 lens, 1/160 second, ISO 400

SHOWCASE
MUSTAFAH ABDULAZIZ

LOCATION: **BERLIN, GERMANY**
WEBSITE: **WWW.MUSTAFAHABDULAZIZ.COM**

I was born in 1986 in New York City, the second of six children and grew up in the mountains of Pennsylvania. A chance encounter at the age of 17 with Richard Avedon's *In The American West* and the idea of visually transporting a viewer into the intimate lives of strangers left a strong impression on me. I have been a member of the international photography collective, MJR, since 2008, and in 2010 I worked as the first contract photographer for *The Wall Street Journal*. In 2011 I moved from New York City to Berlin, where I am currently based.

How did you get into street photography?
I got my start working as a photojournalist for newspapers. This work resembles street-photography. But while on these assignments I began to see that the moments before and after the time I was supposed to be photographing for my paper comprised more reality than what I was hired for.

I call my project "Memory Loss" because I think that so much of what we do and invest in is sometimes forgotten in the monotony of routine. In order to make these photographs I simply needed to put myself into places where I've no reason to be. I take road trips across America. I'm not seeing anything exceptional or you couldn't see yourself if you went out there. I just translate it into something for myself.

What would you say is your style? What makes you stand out?
I try to keep my work simple and responsive. Because I'm interested in connections and disconnects, a part of it is looking for where the line is between me and the subject or environment I'm coming across. I always ask myself, "Would this image be made if I wasn't here?" This process lets me stay honest with what I'm feeling. It's important to question your own motives. I'm constantly questioning mine.

What equipment do you use?
A Mamiya 7II, usually with an 80mm $f/4$ or 65mm $f/4$ lens. It's pretty quiet and compact enough to easily fit into my backpack. I use Kodak Portra 400 film, in 120 format and rate it at ISO 200 and pull ½ of a stop when I develop.

← Ground Zero on the Day Osama bin Laden was Killed by US Special Forces—NYC, USA
Mamiya 7II, 80mm *f*/4 lens, Kodak Portra 400 film rated at 200 and pulled ½ stop

↑ Mo, Daughter of the Owner, Rosalinda's Gentleman's Club—Jamestown, California, USA
Mamiya 7II, 65mm *f*/4 lens, Kodak Portra 400 film rated at 200 and pulled ½ stop

↑ Police Patrol Car—Nazareth, Pennsylvania, USA
Mamiya 7II, 80mm *f*/4 lens, Kodak Portra 400 film rated at 200 and pulled ½ stop

↑ People Await the Arrival of Hurricane Irene—Coney Island, NYC, USA
Mamiya 7II, 80mm *f*/4 lens, Kodak Portra 400 film rated at 200 and pulled ½ stop

↑ Birthday Party at an Upscale Hotel—Queens, NYC, USA
Mamiya 7II, 80mm *f*/4 lens, Kodak Portra 400 film rated at 200 and pulled ½ stop

→ Jamaica, 31, Motel 6—New Mexico, USA
Mamiya 7II, 80mm *f*/4 lens, Kodak Portra 400 film rated at 200 and pulled ½ stop

← Ezekiel, Hell's Kitchen—Manhattan, NYC, USA
Mamiya 7II, 80mm *f*/4 lens, Kodak Portra 400 film rated at 200 and pulled ½ stop

How I made *ESPN Stands in Times Square During the US vs Japan Women's World Cup Match*

This photograph is from Times Square in NYC on the day the USA Women's soccer team played the World Cup match against Japan. Stands had been set up for the public to watch the game on big screens. I'd gone there for an assignment for *The Wall Street Journal* and when I arrived with my digital camera I knew I needed to shoot this for my street project, "Memory Loss." I raced back to my apartment in Brooklyn and grabbed my Mamiya, three rolls of film, and returned just as the second half of the game was starting.

I was struck by all the different combinations of people and moods within this shared experience of watching a football match. The crowd would roar when the US team came close to scoring, and then plunge into silence when the Japanese players regained the ball. I liked the idea of not knowing what the people were watching. By the mood of the crowd I knew what was happening. The man in the middle started to doze off during the end of the match and I knew I had my photograph. Here was a fan who had painted his face red, white, and blue, but had worn a shirt that was for an American football team, the New York Giants. In the middle of NYC, the busiest and maybe loudest part of the city that day, he was falling asleep among a group of total strangers as the experience he came for flashed by.

The Americans lost 3–1 on penalties in extra time. After the wave of excitement had crested, the stands were emptied.

→ **ESPN Stands in Times Square During the US vs Japan Women's World Cup Match—NYC, USA**
Mamiya 7II, 80mm ƒ/4 lens, Kodak Portra 400 film rated at 200 and pulled ½ stop

SHOWCASE
RONYA GALKA

LOCATION: **LONDON, UK**
WEBSITE: **WWW.RONYAGALKA.COM**

My love for street photography ultimately comes from my love of observing people and the desire to celebrate people's individuality. I am very fortunate to live in such a vibrant and fast-moving city: London. Here, on a daily basis you can observe the most surreal and surprising scenes unfold right before your eyes.

How did you get into street photography?
It was only when I started to carry my camera with me on a daily basis a few years ago that I noticed just how many urban moments you come across and are able to isolate from the busy hustle and bustle of life in the city. After just a few first attempts, I was pretty much hooked on street photography and the hunt for ordinary moments happening to ordinary people in everyday situations has now become part of my daily routine.

What would you say is your style? What makes you stand out?
I am not afraid to admit that I shoot with my heart! I would describe my style as emotive and highly subjective—I consider myself a story-teller. All of my street work is candid and unstaged—the scenes that I isolate and capture in the street are very often an expression of my own thoughts, emotions, and concerns at the time. As an example, my ongoing "Rat Race" series focuses on the tiresome routine of workers in the City of London and was initially born out of radical changes at my own workplace, and the ensuing feeling of helplessness and frustration that I was feeling at the time. The common thread that runs through all my pictures is the human sentiments that make everyday life so magical: love, joy, sadness, friendship, solitude—feelings that all of us can relate to. Visually much of my work is centered around shadow-play and the use of silhouettes.

What equipment do you use?
Sometimes I shoot street with my DSLR, but since most of my work involves getting up close and personal with my subjects, in order to stay "invisible" I prefer to shoot street with my favorite all-round street camera, my Ricoh GX200.

→ Every Exit is an Entrance Somewhere Else—London, UK
Sony DSC-P100, 8mm ƒ/5.6 lens, ISO 100

↓ Going Home—London, UK
Canon PowerShot S3 IS, 21mm ƒ/5.6 lens

↓ It Must be Monday Morning— London, UK
Sony DSC-P100, 9mm ƒ/3.2 lens, ISO 100

↑ A Bug's Life—Paris, France
Ricoh GX200, 5mm ƒ/7.2 lens, ISO 200

↑ The Aim of Life is to Live— London, UK
Sony DSC-P100, 8mm ƒ/5.6 lens, ISO 100

↑ One Day I'll Fly Away— London, UK
Sony DSC-P100, 24mm ƒ/5.2 lens, ISO 100

↑ The Rat Race—London, UK
Canon PowerShot S3 IS, 8mm ƒ/3.2 lens, ISO 100

How I made *I Don't Care What the Weatherman Says*
This picture was taken on one of my many walks through London. More often than not, when I go out to shoot street, I don't have a set idea or plan of where I will go or the type of shot that I might capture on that day. For me part of the excitement is all about wandering through the streets to see what scenes may unfold. I prefer to be on the move all the time. I don't stay stationary for too long. There are two reasons for this. Firstly, in a fast-paced city like London, people rush from one place to the next and if you want to blend in you need to move with the same pace that they do. Secondly, I am convinced that when I loiter and stay around in the same spot people are aware of me photographing them, which inhibits my street work. The moment people become aware of me shooting them I stop. My work is about candid moments and someone who is acting up for the camera just does not appeal to me.

Someone once said that "Luck is when preparation meets opportunity" and that quote is certainly very apt for street photography. As long as you observe your surroundings, and are aware of the people around you, you are already halfway there to "receive" street shots. Scenes unfold on the street ALL THE TIME (there is no such thing as the "right place and right time.") As long as you are prepared, have your camera on you at all times with your shutter finger ready, you are sure to "harvest" a few shots. And that is exactly what happened with this shot. After a few hours of unsuccessful street shooting, I was on my way home. It started to rain quite heavily and just as I walked across Trafalgar Square, the couple in front of me started to hug, seemingly oblivious to the pouring rain. The moment only lasted a few seconds, but the shot that I captured stayed with me in the form of a lovely scene of friendship and love. Often these moments present themselves to you and things come together right in front of your lens and all you really have to do is press the shutter. It's a great feeling when things just come together for the briefest of all moments when you have the perfect view and angle for the shot, and even before you look at your screen you know that you have captured a memorable street shot.

SHOWCASE
SEAMUS TRAVERS

LOCATION: **DUBLIN, IRELAND**
WEBSITE: **WWW.SEAMUSTRAVERS.COM**

My dad was a photographer, and when I was 16 he gave me a camera. I wandered around aimlessly and took photos in downtown Dublin. When I went to college, I studied animation and neglected photography for a while. It was only in my late 20s that I picked up a camera again. I am a portrait photographer by profession, but when I am not in the studio, I am making photos on the streets.

How did you get into street photography?
After leaving college I started working as a retoucher and graphic designer for other photographers, and I was exposed to different styles of photography. What appealed to me about street photography, was it seemed at the time to be the most challenging. It was not until I saw a competition for street photography online to win a rangefinder, that I started to passionately roam Dublin for street images week-in week-out. I think in my first two years I wore out a few pairs of shoes doing this.

What would you say is your style? What makes you stand out?
It's hard to put into words if I have a style as such. For me it still starts with an idea. Usually I pre-visualize an absurd or strange moment taking place in an ordinary situation. I prefer absurdity, over realist photography. It's difficult to put into words, but more often than not, if I go out roaming a town or city with a positive attitude, events fall into place—minor extraordinary moments in the ordinary.

In the editing process I'm very self-critical. Shooting film allows me to be even more frugal in my image selection. Shooting digital I feel would not allow me the same discipline.

What equipment do you use?
A Leica M6 with a 35mm wide-angle lens. For panoramic street shots, I use a Hasselblad Xpan. It uses 35mm film, but rather than taking a 24mm x 35mm frame, it shoots a 24mm x 65mm image. Although built for landscape photography, its portable size makes it ideal for street. I also use a Nikon F3 SLR, with a waist-level viewfinder—useful for hip shots.

↓ Barbershop—Dublin, Ireland
Leica M6, Zeiss Biogon, ZM 35mm ƒ/2
lens, Fuji Neopan 1600

**↓ Bareback Horse Riding—
Dublin, Ireland**
Leica M6, Elmar 50mm ƒ/2.8 lens, Kodak
Portra 160VC

**← Trieste—
Italy**
Leica M6, Zeiss
Biogon, ZM 35mm
ƒ/2 lens, Kodak
Tri-X

**← Market—
Yerevan,
Armenia**
Hasselblad Xpan,
Carl Zeiss 45mm
lens, Fuji 400
Pro-H

↑ Dublin—Ireland
Nikon F3, 50mm ƒ/1.8 lens, Fuji Neopan
400, developed in D76

**←← Brick
Wall—
Arizona, USA**
Nikon D200,
17–55mm lens,
ISO 100

**← Family Street
Scene—Dublin,
Ireland**
Leica M6, Zeiss
Biogon ZM 35mm
ƒ/2 lens, Ilford
Delta 400

How I made *Vertical Panorama*

I had been strolling this area of London with my Xpan camera with the idea of getting a vertical panoramic image. London, with its high-rise buildings, is a lot more diverse than Dublin (a much smaller city), and especially suitable for the vertical format. The vast majority of panoramic photos tend to be horizontal landscape images so a vertical image is much more unusual.

It was a very overcast day in January when I made this photo. The light was so dull I added an orange filter to the lens to increase the contrast on the black-and-white film. I was shooting ISO 400 film, and I had to increase my aperture by one-and-a-half stops to compensate for the loss of light due to the colored filter. Ideally two stops would have been better as I like a little more exposure on my negatives. However, the light was so dull that even using 400 speed film, it would have given me under the 1/125 second shutter speed that I wanted to freeze movement. With ƒ/8 for depth of field to keep foreground and background sharp, I got a sense of size and scale that is important when shooting panoramic frames.

The poster of the long figures caught my eye; I walked around it to see if I could juxtapose it with something. I saw a large group of pigeons ahead. I walked slowly around the birds, so as not to disturb them. I prefocused the rangefinder into the area with the highest concentration of birds and waited for someone to walk by, causing them to fly up into the air.

In the distance I could see a man holding a mattress. I waited for him to come into frame and photographed him as he walked below the poster. That image was not scanned or used as the man in the suit in the featured image has an annoyed expression due to the birds flying around him. The movie poster is for a film called *Valkyrie*, and the birds in flight evoke thoughts of the Wagner opera, *Ride of the Valkyries*.

The 45mm lens, which is near normal focal length on an ordinary 24mm x 35mm frame, is the equivalent of a 21mm wide-angle lens when being shot on the panoramic 24mm x 65mm format. Having such a wide view allowed me to point

the camera in the direction of the poster without the man in the foreground realizing that I was photographing him. Nothing was said and there was no eye contact made.

This is one of the rare times where I waited for elements to fall into place. In terms of street photographers, I put them into two categories. Hunters or gatherers. Hunters walk around until they find a scene and capture it instantly as it unfolds around them. Gatherers find a spot and then wait for something to happen. I mostly make images in the former category. I am too impatient to wait a few minutes before moving on. While no one method is necessarily better than the other, everything depends on the final image.

← **Vertical Panorama—London, UK**
Hasselblad Xpan, Carl Zeiss 45mm lens with orange filter,
Ilford Delta 400

SHOWCASE
SHOWCASE
SEVERIN KOLLER

LOCATION: **VIENNA, AUSTRIA**
WEBSITE: **WWW.SEVERINKOLLER.COM**

I was born in 1986 close to Vienna, Austria. After graduating, I started studying at the Academy of Fine Arts Vienna in 2005. Since 2005 I've been working as a freelance photographer for advertising, magazines, and newspapers.

How did you get into street photography?
A photographer friend let me borrow his Leica M6 with a 35mm Summicron. After using it for about two weeks, I decided to buy one and since then I've been shooting street almost every day.

What would you say is your style? What makes you stand out?
I'd say I have two approaches to street. One aims at the story being told in a single frame and the other for a larger body of photographs that works as a whole. I wouldn't say that one attempt is better than the other, but it's often the case that those photos that have the aura of a "perfect" capture attract more attention. For my portfolio I have a strict selection of images in this category, while when I blog or work on a series,

I post many more photos that create a story when seen together.

What equipment do you use?
I've been shooting street with a Leica M6 and 35mm (focal length) lenses for about six years. I shoot solely film because I shot street on film from the beginning. I think it is important to have a signature as a photographer, so I have been using the same films, developer, and focal length for street since I started out. When shooting portraits I stick to one camera and one lens. Film has its own imminent characteristics while digital will always need some post-processing in order to "come alive." When I shoot on film I get less distracted too. Everything I do is about creating that photo and when I shoot I focus on the next image without checking my display or browsing through the images and deleting some. I believe that this different workflow produces better photos for me.

← **Auditorium—Museum Island, Berlin, Germany**
Leica M6, 35mm ƒ/2 lens, 1/500 second, Kodak Tri-X 400 film

↘ **LA Jesus—Hollywood Boulevard, Los Angeles, USA**
Leica M8.2, 24mm ƒ/1.4 lens, 1/60 second, ISO 640

→ **Mariahilfer Street—Vienna, Austria**
Leica M6, 35mm ƒ/2 lens, 1/500 second, Kodak PlusX 125 film

← ← **Lexington Avenue—New York, USA**
Leica M6, 35mm ƒ/2 lens, 1/250 second, Kodak Tri-X 400 film

← **Subway Station—Los Angeles, USA**
Leica M6, 35mm ƒ/2 lens, 1/60 second, Kodak Tri-X 400 film

↑↑ **Oberbaum Bridge—Berlin, Germany**
Leica M6, 35mm ƒ/2 lens, 1/4 second, Kodak Tri-X 400 film

↑ **Manhattan—New York, USA**
Leica M6, 35mm ƒ/2 lens, 1/500 second, Kodak PlusX 125 film

How I made *Grand Central Station*

To explain the thoughts I have while I take these photos is almost impossible, because it is instinctive—there is no time to think about taking a photo, the moment would be gone if you did. So here is an exception. I saw the potential of a good street shot and waited for it.

The Grand Central Station terminal in New York isn't a very bright station. The famous photographs by Edward Lunch and John Collier, where sunbeams light up the whole station, were taken in the 1940s before high rises were built around it. Today, the gigantic windows in the main hall don't deliver any direct sunlight. Most of the photographs we see show less contrast due to the softer and duller light that fills the station. The only spots of light in the hall were tiny reflections of a skyscraper's window. So I walked to this illuminated area to meter on the light for the right exposure.

For this photo I had a shutter speed of 1/125th second at ISO 125 and aperture ƒ/2.8. Ideally I would have used more sensitive film, such as ISO 400, or if shooting digital, would have chosen a higher ISO, because ƒ/2.8 requires exact focusing and stopping down to ƒ/4.0 would have resulted in a 1/60th second shutter speed, which would have been slightly too slow for a photo like this one, in which people were moving.

An image like this only delivers the desired effect if the exposure is dead on. Of course, with a digital camera you can just try several exposures and see which one works best. The better learning experience though, is to meter with fixed, "generally useful" ISO values (between 100 and 800) so that you remember certain settings. Once you've memorized some of these general settings, you will be much quicker and make less mistakes when taking photos. For example, in a subway, you will need an aperture of between ƒ/1.4 and ƒ/2.8, and ISO 400 plus. So entering an underground station with the right settings already set on your camera will save time when you see something you want to photograph.

In general it is always helpful to meter every time the light has changed, so that you have your camera ready—if you have to start adjusting the controls on your camera the moment will be gone.

GLOSSARY

35mm Camera A camera that takes 35mm film size.

35mm Film A film with width 35mm (also called 135 film). This is the most popular and common type of film available.

Aperture Aperture is the hole in a lens that light travels through to reach the film or the camera's sensor. Controlling the size of this hole controls the amount of light entering the lens.

Burn A photographic process to darken parts of an image.

Channel Mixer A powerful tool used in monochrome conversion allowing you to control how much of the three channel colors—red, green, and blue—contribute to the grayscale brightness of the image. This in turn can transform a washed-out black-and-white image into one with richer tones and contrast.

Creative Commons License The creative commons license allows others to use your images for free, with a link to your name or website, thereby attributing you as the artist.

C-41 Processing A chemical process used to process color film.

Crop Factor Most digital cameras have a crop factor that is caused by a smaller sensor that crops the lens' image, thereby reducing the potential frame size of an image. For example, a 50mm lens with a crop factor of 1.6 will actually perform as a 75mm lens. Film cameras are full-frame meaning there is no crop factor to take into account. Some DSLRs are full-frame, but are much more expensive than those with a crop factor.

Curves The curves tool is a significant one in photo editing software that affects tones and contrast—two elements central to the aesthetic qualities of an image.

Decisive Moment A term coined by street photographer Henri Cartier-Bresson and used widely in the world of street photography to describe the idea of aspects of a photograph coming together to form a moment that tells a story.

Depth of Field DOF is the distance between elements within a frame, with the focal point on a particular element. A shallow DOF has the focus on a subject with progressive blurriness around it, while a large DOF allows for many elements to be in focus.

Dodge A photographic process to lighten parts of an image.

DSLR and SLR A single-lens reflex camera uses a moving mirror system and when you look through the viewfinder, you are actually looking through prisms and mirrors, reflecting exactly what the lens is seeing. So in essence you are looking through the lens (TTL), allowing you to see precisely what will be captured on camera, whether film, or on a memory card for a DSLR.

Exposure A combination of the aperture and shutter speed. To produce the correct exposure, you need to ensure the shutter speed and aperture are both set correctly, and this is based on the amount of light available.

Grain/Noise A side effect of using a high ISO in low light, illustrated by a grainy look consisting of specks.

ISO This is the sensitivity of film to light, and in digital photography is the sensitivity of the camera's sensor. Low ISOs are ideal for where there is a lot of light available, and high ISOs are ideal for low-light situations. The higher the ISO, the more grain or noise is produced.

JPEG A universal image file format recognized and supported by all computers and photo-displaying devices.

Juxtaposition The positioning of elements next to one another.

Leica A popular rangefinder brand used by the early pioneers of street photography, and by many today.

Light Meter The light meter indicates when the exposure is correct either within the viewfinder of the camera, or in the case of an external light meter, on the device itself.

Lomography A photography movement using cheap, plastic film cameras such as a Holga, producing surreal, dream-like images with effects such as vignetting, and unusual saturation and contrast.

Manual Camera/Mode A fully manual camera or using manual mode is one where settings may or must be set by the photographer manually, such as focusing, shutter speed, and aperture. Conversely, automatic mode allows the camera to select the most appropriate settings for a given situation, eliminating the need for the photographer to do this. Semi-automatic modes are available allowing photographers to control some but not all of the settings.

Medium Format Camera A camera that takes a larger film size than the usual 35mm—typically 120mm and 220mm.

Micro Four Thirds A compact digital camera with interchangeable lenses. It's superior to a point-and-shoot digital camera, but differs from a DSLR as it is mirrorless, making it more compact.

Motion Blur When a slow shutter speed is used with moving subjects, this causes the subjects to appear blurry and gives a ghost-like effect—a result of the long exposure used.

Prime Lens A prime lens is one with a fixed focal length that cannot zoom in and out. It is generally a fast, high-quality lens allowing for a very shallow DOF and usage in low light. It is also generally quite compact—making it ideal for street

Pushing and Pulling Film Pushing or pulling film allows photographers to make a particular film type behave like that of a faster or slower film. When it comes to developing the film, it will need to be developed for a longer or shorter amount of time, or at a higher or lower temperature than perhaps the film was originally intended for.

Rangefinder camera A camera that contains a rangefinding device, which is a distance-determination mechanism to bring a scene into focus, as opposed to looking through the lens to focus as is the case with SLRs. A common rangefinder uses a prism and mirror whose angles can be manually adjusted using a movable ring, to align two superimposed images together to create the perfect focus. This is considered to be the most ideal camera for street photography.

Raw A very large file format that allows much more flexibility and room for maneuver in post-processing images. It contains untouched Raw information straight from the digital camera's sensor. Raw files must always be processed with customized software in order to be universally viewable.

Rule of Thirds A common rule of thumb in photography dictating that a frame should be split into nine sections, with the main subject(s) placed along the lines or at the intersections. The sections should contain three lines spaced equally, horizontally, and vertically. Ideally, the main subject would be positioned in a space the size of one third of the frame.

Shooting From The Hip A method of shooting where the photographer does not look through the viewfinder of the camera, but instead shoots "blindly" without being able to see exactly what is being captured. It's a useful approach if you are trying to be inconspicuous.

Shutter Speed The shutter of any camera is closed, until you click to make an image. When you do this, the shutter opens and closes for a period of time known as the shutter speed, allowing light to reach the film or camera's sensor.

TLR A twin-lens reflex camera, which differs from an SLR in that it has two lenses of the same focal length; one to take the picture, and one for the viewfinder. The viewfinder is at the top of the camera and often looked through at waist-level, making picture-taking less obvious.

Zoom Lens A lens that has a varied focal length allowing a photographer to take a closer crop of a scene without moving.

INDEX

ACKNOWLEDGMENTS

I'd like to thank the team at Ilex Photo, and in particular Adam Juniper, for letting me write about a subject that is a passion of mine. Street photography deserves far more attention than it currently gets, and you have provided me with the perfect outlet to talk about it. A big thank you also to Natalia Price-Cabrera, Managing Editor at Ilex Photo, for doing a wonderful editing job, and taking my countless suggestions and opinions onboard.

A massive thanks to all the contributors—Kishan Chandarana for his expertise and insight into the laws surrounding street photography (which I learned a huge amount from) and to all the photographers who have done a sterling job—Antonio, Brian, Charlotte, Claire, Danny, Felix, Ferhat, Mustafah, Ronya, Seamus, and Severin. You guys are absolutely awesome and inspirational, and I urge anyone reading this to check out your photography online. You are artists that anyone with a love of photography can and should learn from.

Thank you to everyone who supported me throughout the writing of this book—colleagues, friends, and family. You encouraged and helped me in all manner of ways. In particular, I can't thank James Bardolph enough for his invaluable input and honest opinions. Moreover, I essentially hijacked his equipment, without which this book would not have been possible!

Lastly, thank you to anyone reading this book—I hope that you've been inspired to shoot street and will contribute to keeping this wonderful genre of photography alive for many years to come.